My Life With Shelter Dogs

My Life With Shelter Dogs

JOHN HUH

Copyright © 2020 by John Huh.

ISBN: Hardcover   978-1-7960-9049-9
       Softcover   978-1-7960-9048-2
       eBook   978-1-7960-9047-5

All rights reserved. No part of this book may be reproduced or transmitted in any form or by any means, electronic or mechanical, including photocopying, recording, or by any information storage and retrieval system, without permission in writing from the copyright owner.

Any people depicted in stock imagery provided by Getty Images are models, and such images are being used for illustrative purposes only.
Certain stock imagery © Getty Images.

Print information available on the last page.

Rev. date: 02/26/2020

To order additional copies of this book, contact:
Xlibris
1-888-795-4274
www.Xlibris.com
Orders@Xlibris.com
809983

CONTENTS

Preface vii
Acknowledgements..ix

Chapter 1   How It All Started 1
Chapter 2   T-Bone..3
Chapter 3   Zeke 5
Chapter 4   Scrappy AKA Einstein 9
Chapter 5   Stella 13
Chapter 6   Bo Duke 17
Chapter 7   Blossom 19
Chapter 8   Bella 23
Chapter 9   Lillie 25
Chapter 10   Jessie 29
Chapter 11   Sky 33
Chapter 12   Pretty Girl 35
Chapter 13   Longshot 39
Chapter 14   Lucas 43
Chapter 15   Patches 45
Chapter 16   Sammy 49
Chapter 17   Bailey 51
Chapter 18   Lola 55
Chapter 19   Lyla 57
Chapter 20   Max 61
Chapter 21   Banjo 69
Chapter 22   The Puppy That Would 73
Chapter 23   Sissy 75

Chapter 24 Diamond and Blitz 79
Chapter 25 Diesel, Rosa, and Katie 81
Chapter 26 Charlie Girl 85
Chapter 27 Puppy Litter Number 1 87
Chapter 28 Puppy Litter Number 2 89
Chapter 29 Animal Control Rescue Dogs 91

Preface

This book is the accounting of how I became involved with shelter dogs and rescued fifty-five of them from high-kill shelters or situations that could have led to death by cruel circumstances or euthanasia.

This story is about not only of these fifty-five dogs but also of dogs that were in shelters but desperately needed help to cope with shelter life. It also describes how dogs with issues were handled so they could learn to deal with their issues and become family members and lead normal lives. It is also about abused dogs and how to get them to trust a human again.

This book is dedicated to my own dog, Scrappy, whom I rescued hours before he was to be euthanized for biting people. He was a fearful, abused dog and didn't trust people. We built his trust on his terms, and eight years later, he is very much loved and part of our family.

Acknowledgements

Outer Banks SPCA and Staff
Outer Banks SPCA Director John Graves
Virginia Beach SPCA and Staff
Fearful Dogs - Debbie Jacobs
Darlene Zacharias adopting Zeke, one of my first rescues
Tami Willis adopting Blossom, another early rescue
Eastern Shore of Virginia, Animal Hospital Dr. Paula Cameron
Roanoke Island Animal Clinic Dr. Burkart
Eastern Shore of Virginia, Animal Control Melfa, Virginia
Without permission from John Graves, much
of this would not have been possible!

Chapter 1
How It All Started

In 2004, I retired and relocated to the Eastern Shore of Virginia. I started volunteering building houses for Habitat for Humanity and learned a lot about basic carpentry skills and how to fix things in regard to construction.

A neighbor of mine was on the board of directors for the local Society for the Prevention of Cruelty to Animals (SPCA), and when she found out what I was doing, she asked if a group of us could take care of some badly needed repairs at the local SPCA.

I visited the SPCA to understand what was needed and told them I felt sure that we could gather the help needed to handle most of their issues. I did tell them that I did not want to get involved with any of their dogs as it seemed so depressing to see them in cages, pleading for attention. That was agreed to, and before long, we were cleaning up their issues.

What I had not counted on was my own weakness in regard to getting involved with dogs that so desperately needed a little attention. In a short time, I found myself playing with them in the outside play yards or sitting with them in their kennels. I was slowly slipping into an uncontrollable status of trying to save the lives of these poor creatures and, better yet, find forever loving homes to live out the rest of their lives in.

Little did I realize how involved this would get and how emotional the ups and downs could get.

My first rescue attempt was a complete failure and ended up with the dog being euthanized. He was a big boy named Dreyfuss, a Mastiff mix breed, and he didn't like one of the staff members. I would sit in his kennel and pet him for hours, and we became buddies. Recognizing that there were issues, I searched and found a rescue that said they would take him. A time and date were set, and I felt we were on the verge of saving this guy's life. The date came and went and no rescue. Calls went unanswered, and staff felt the situation was getting unsafe, and he was euthanized.

I was sick over it, but there was another dog there in a very similar situation. A staff member openly admitted to being afraid of him, so I knew what was going to happen based on my very recent past experience. Again, I called around and found a rescue that said they would look at him and decide. Learning from my first attempt with a rescue, I decided I would bring the dog to them, and we would go from there. All was agreed to, including a time and meeting place, and I packed up our white German Shepherd, named T-Bone, and off we went. This one was successful, and more of his story will follow in a later chapter.

By now, I was recognizing that I was getting pretty well hooked on working with shelter dogs and decided I needed some help to learn more about how to work with these dogs. It was suggested by the local SPCA Director that I visit the VB SPCA and spend some time with them, and they would be willing to teach me more about shelter dogs, including handling fearful dogs, enrichment, clicker training, and doing aggression assessments.

I made the trip down there, explained my situation, and was greeted with open arms, and training began almost immediately. I made the hour-and-a-half trip down there twice a week and, as I got more involved, made even more trips there weekly. I also found an excellent source on the handling of fearful dogs with a person by the name of Debbie Jacobs, who is the author of a book on handling fearful dogs and has a website and Facebook group on fearful dogs as well.

I have done my best to document my experiences with each dog and also follow up with pictures in as many cases as I could. The following chapters will be dog-specific with the exception of very similar circumstances; multiple dogs may be covered in the same chapter.

Chapter 2

T-Bone

I was volunteering at a local SPCA in Virginia and had just lost a dog that I had a wonderful relationship with. He was a Mastiff, and his name was Dreyfuss. He was a big boy, and I could tell that staff was very leery of him. I got involved with him for precisely that reason.

About that time, another big dog came in from animal control by the name of T-Bone. He was a white German Shepherd and a big dog. His story was that when a local supermarket opened one morning, T-Bone was found inside the store. He had helped himself to the meat counter, hence the name T-Bone.

I was there one day with T-Bone, and one of the staff members openly admitted that she was afraid of him. I saw the handwriting on the wall, so I started looking for a rescue and found a German Shepherd rescue in VB. This time instead of having them come up to look at him, I took him down to them. We met at the VB SPCA, and there were two women there from the rescue. One was a dog trainer, and she took the leash and worked on some obedience and leash walking with T-Bone and liked what she saw.

It was decided that we would take him over to the police barracks to see if there was any potential for police work, and it was quickly determined that T-Bone was "too sweet" for that line of duty. They did, however, give us a demonstration of a not-so-sweet dog, and it was an amazing thing to see.

So it was decided that T-Bone would go into a foster and be put up for adoption. I turned him over and left for home, feeling at least he now had a chance to make it.

I stayed in touch with the rescue and was sent a message before long that he had been adopted and was living outside the Washington, D.C., area. They also sent a couple of beautiful pictures of him taken by a professional photographer, which I cherish.

This was the first dog that I had a hand in saving. I could see things were headed the wrong way at the SPCA with a staff member openly admitting she was afraid of him. That young lady soon decided that working in an SPCA was not something that she could really do, and thankfully, no lives were lost during that process.

Chapter 3

Zeke

There is a small shelter in Virginia that works very hard to place their dogs as most all shelters do. They have volunteers that help at the shelter, spending time with the dogs, and work on making their stay as comfortable as time in a shelter can be. The inherent issue with volunteers and shelter dogs is getting attached on both sides. This is a short story of one of those situations.

A Yellow Lab made his way into the shelter. I can't remember if he was a stray or surrendered, but he was not kenneling very well. As a volunteer, I started to spend time with the dog, and life started to become a little bit more bearable for the dog, named Spencer, later to be renamed Zeke.

Spencer was the second shelter dog that I got involved with that was going to be euthanized. I did lose the first one but made a promise to myself that I would do all I could to not let it happen again. Terminal sickness or severe aggression, I can understand, but other than those two reasons, I will do all I can to stop euthanasia.

This took place at a local SPCA in Virginia. He is what I called one of my dogs, meaning I was already spending time with him. We went on vacation for two weeks, and upon our return, I was told by shelter staff that he was scheduled for euthanasia that afternoon. The reason was that he had developed intolerance for staying in a kennel and displayed behavior that was typical for dogs that are diagnosed as "kennel crazy." Typical behavior for these dogs is bouncing off kennel side walls or spinning in their kennels.

Zeke was spinning so badly that he had worn his hind nails down past the quick, and they were bleeding. He was clearly suffering.

I asked and was granted permission to take him to my vet to see if there might be some medical issue we were missing. I can remember as we were leaving the shelter, I knew that there was no way I would bring him back. We would somehow find a way to deal with it.

I took him to my vet, Dr. Paula. I can still remember standing in front of her, almost feeling like a little boy and his dog that was in big trouble. We must have been a very pitiful sight as I couldn't hold back as a tear ran down my cheek. Dr. Paula suggested a chance for him.

Zeke was a young male, probably about a year old. She said if I would pay to neuter him, he could stay at the hospital free of charge until I found a home for him. I called the shelter, and they agreed, so we had a deal.

He was neutered within a day or so, and I would come every day and spend time with him. We would play outside, take walks, and just hang out together. They had these plastic chairs in the yards that I would sit on, and he would manage to crawl under them, which was a task because he was a big boy.

We put the word out about a dog needing a home, and one day, while I was at the hospital, I had a phone call. A lady heard about him and wanted to come and see him, which she did. We took him out and spent time with him until it was time for her to leave. She said she would be back the next day. I felt very good about the way it went and just took a wait-and-see attitude.

The next day went even better than the first day as she brought some treats with her, and he was a good boy, sitting and staying. We had another visit, this time with her dog that was very old, and things went very well there also.

It was decision time, and she decided to take him. It was over the Fourth of July, and they had plans, so she said she would come for him after the holiday, which she did. I was delighted as she really was a dog person and saw what I saw in him. She wondered why I didn't take him myself, and I said we already had our Maggie, a Yellow Lab, and I felt one dog was enough, especially one big dog.

A couple of weeks later, I was invited to go over and visit. He was doing very well. We had a great visit, and when I got into my truck to leave, he crawled under it and wouldn't come out. Darlene went in and got a treat, which he came out for, ate it, and went back under the truck. This time she lured him out with another treat, and she grabbed his collar and brought him into the house. I remember him standing behind the glass door watching me as I backed out of the driveway. I didn't realize that I had bonded that much with him.

Years have passed, and I still visit with him, and sometimes I bring my Maggie along. They play, running around the backyard, jumping off their dock, swimming, and have a great time together. He is a big boy now weighing one hundred pounds and seems to remember me like it was yesterday. He loves men and has really bonded with Zach, Darlene's husband. Zeke is very mischievous, getting into a little trouble from time to time, but is very much loved.

Attached are some pictures. One in particular shows just how mischievous he can be. They had work done on their porch and had picked all the scrap pieces of wood and put them in a wheelbarrow. Attached is a picture of him in the wheelbarrow, unloading it.

As you look at these pictures and you realize how close he came to be being euthanized, it really makes you wonder about some of the decisions that are made about euthanasia. At the Outer Banks SPCA, dogs are only euthanized for illness or severe aggression. They don't hold an inventory of unsprayed or unneutered animals, and they understand sometimes simply a location change can make the difference.

Of the two dogs in my truck, my Maggie is the one with the pink nose.

Several years have passed since the above happened with Zeke. I did see Darlene, his owner, one day, and she suggested that I come and pay him a visit.

We entered the house, and what happened next was quite a surprise for me. To say he remembered me is a huge understatement. He went absolutely nuts, jumping on the furniture, and was all over me. He also knocked over a table with a house plant on it. We finally both settled down and enjoyed each other's company.

I asked a dog behaviorist about this, and she said that he considered me his savior and did not or would not forget me, and that has certainly turned out to be true.

Chapter 4

Scrappy AKA Einstein

I will start with a brief history of Scrappy as I know it and carry it through present day.

It was back in 2011 when I was told about some hoarder dogs that had been confiscated from Elkins, West Virginia. It seems someone had thirty small dogs, Chihuahua and Terrier mixes, that were contained in a single wide trailer. Conditions were so bad, with feces and urine, that rescue folks had to wear breathing apparatus to make the rescue. Once rescued, the dogs were cleaned up and split up, sending sixteen to the Norfolk SPCA and fourteen to the VB SPCA.

I was contacted as a possible volunteer to help with the ones at the VB SPCA as I was already a volunteer there. The overall responsibility was assigned to a very kind young woman who worked at the VB SPCA. I was told to look for her when I got there, and she would take it from there.

Because of what they had been through and the fact that they were very fearful, they were housed in the clinic area of the SPCA, meaning they were in their own room that had their own kennels, not mainstreamed with other shelter dogs. I met Cara and was told I would have to suit up. This meant wearing a smock, shoe covers, and something on my head. Also, I had to wash my hands before we entered the room.

I was not prepared for what I was about to see. A total of fourteen little dogs divided up three or four to a kennel, all pressed into the farthest back corner of the kennels and all trembling, not knowing what was going to happen to them next. I was heartbroken. I went to the first kennel, opened the door, and sat in the doorway, talking to them. I did the same to all four kennels and was totally ignored by all the dogs as they were just too scared to react positively.

I can't remember the frequency of my visits as I was an hour and a half away, but I did go often, and between staff and volunteers, we started to make some progress. There was one little dude that started to show that he was the dominant one. His name was Einstein, and with his shaggy appearance, he even looked like Einstein. He began to venture out of the back corners and move to the front of the kennel. He also started to display some dominance over the others and kept them in the back of the kennel while he roamed the front area of the kennel. When I opened the door, he would quickly retreat to the rear of the kennel, but he started to eat treats that were tossed near him.

We would cut hot dogs up into very tiny pieces and try and lure them from the back of the kennels, but other than Einstein, they wouldn't eat them until we left.

Einstein got to the point that they had to put him in his own kennel as he was really picking on his kennel mates. Also, as people were starting to handle these dogs, Einstein bit someone.

Time was going by, and they had been there nearly two months. Some of them came around nicely, and some were getting adopted. As a matter of fact, we were down to seven of the fourteen. There was concern that some would not make it because of their feral nature. I was spending more time with Einstein because he was getting himself in more trouble. One of the staff members brought him home for an evening, and he bit her twice, once in the stomach.

I started to work on getting him to climb on my lap by luring him up there with tiny pieces of hot dog. He would climb, take the hot dog, and run back to a kennel corner. Meanwhile, there was another bit incident.

Then one day he really surprised me by climbing on my lap, taking the hot dog, and instead of running off with it, he ate it and curled up and stayed on my lap. I can't even begin to tell you the emotions that I was feeling at that time. I left for the day feeling that I had reached the trust point with him, and that was a huge step.

I went in for my next visit and found out that the decision had been made to euthanize the remainder of the dogs there. They were considered feral, and it was felt they could not be adopted out. One dog named Buckin was transferred to Norfolk, and I believe that left six. Faced with this turn of events, I had to decide, and I asked and was given permission to take one of them. I had spent time with Hugo and Einstein, and it was felt by staff that I would have the most luck with Einstein.

That was over eight years ago, and it's been quite a ride with him. He ran away once, being gone for two weeks before getting him back. I believe the total number of bites were logged as five while at the SPCA. He bit me once, when I foolishly tried to put a ThunderShirt on him in the vet's office. What was I thinking?

All in all, it's been a wonderful experience. He loves our Yellow Lab, Maggie. She tries to ignore him, but on two separate occasions, she has gotten between him and another dog that went after him, and they backed off as she meant business.

This brings us to where we are with him today. Charlene changed his name to Scrappy, which fits him perfectly, although the shades of Einstein show through from time to time. It seems he really has Charlene figured out and can play her like a fiddle when he wants to. This usually happens at feeding and grooming time. He will only allow half of his body to be groomed, and at feeding time, he makes Charlene stand on her head trying to get him to eat. She adds cheese or chicken breast or both and begs him to eat. Sometimes he will, and sometimes he won't.

My approach is somewhat different and works nearly all the time, when Charlene is not home. I prepare his food and give it to him. If he doesn't eat, I just walk away and leave him and it there. After a few minutes, he almost always realizes nothing else is coming, so he will go and eat. I have also been known to let Maggie eat it. Tough love, I believe it's called.

Dogs are amazing creatures. Rescue dogs or dogs that have suffered at the hands of cruel people are very special dogs. If I kept all the dogs that I have had a hand in rescuing, I would own over fifty dogs now. I will admit to wanting number 3, but it is just not to be.

So for now, I will enjoy my little family, other people's dogs, and shelter dogs and continue to learn and help as many dogs as I can as it is truly a privilege to be given the opportunity to do so.

Chapter 5

Stella

Stella is a little girl Pit mix. She was found by vet staff in a ditch on the Virginia Eastern Shore, so emaciated she could barely walk. She had a scar on her neck, where the chain grew into it. Her ears were eaten by flies, and she was truly a bag of bones. She had many litters of puppies by the looks of her, and no one knows what their fate was. It is speculated that whoever had her saw death was near and, rather than have to bury her, turned her loose to die in the surrounding woods.

As fate would have it, the husband of a vet tech saw her in the ditch and went home and told his wife. Soon, a couple of vet techs were at the scene, trying to get her loaded up to take back to the clinic. She was near death and could barely walk, so they were able to load her up without incident. They fed her and made her as comfortable as possible and left her for the evening. This might have been the first time she was ever in a building, out of the outdoor elements.

It was decided that she would remain at the vet's office and start the rehab process. It turns out she didn't like other dogs and was very food aggressive, which was no surprise, given her condition.

A short time passed, and it was recognized there was a problem with her as she was not passing anything. They went in and did surgery and found a blockage in her intestines of pieces of a corncob. That was taken care of, and while they were in there, they spayed her.

I was at the vet for a routine visit with one of my dogs and was told about her. I asked if I could see her, and we became instant friends. I was amazed that a dog this badly treated could be so affectionate toward a human. I brought my dog home and returned to her and spent the rest of the day with her. As a matter of fact, I was so taken by her I spent the next month with her. We took long walks together, and I spent time just sitting in a shady area, just talking to her and petting her. I also started feeding her by hand to grow the relationship and get rid of any food aggression that she might have had with people. She let me do absolutely anything with her, and the relationship was growing fast, also my love for her.

She was recovering nicely, but we knew we had to get her off the Shore for her to stand a chance. I took her to the Outer Banks for a day trip, and we also went to the VB SPCA for a visit. I felt she would have the best chance at the Norfolk SPCA because they are a no-kill shelter. The Shelter Director was very nice to us and told us they were full, but they would put her on a waiting list. I accepted that because I was running out of options.

One month later, I got the call to bring her in. I felt guilty leaving her, but I knew I couldn't take her, and this was the best possible chance she would get. I stayed away from her for about eight or nine months and finally had to see her. I didn't know what to expect when we met but was pleasantly surprised that she remembered me and was all over me with kisses and trying to get onto my lap. This again was an unbelievable experience.

I saw her several times after this with always the same reception, but she had been there for about eleven months without any serious inquiries. Then yesterday morning, I was working on the computer, and an e-mail popped up from Kari, the Shelter Director, titled "Good News!"

I am not at all ashamed to say that even without opening the e-mail, tears came to my eyes. She had been through so much, and could she possibly have made it?

I will admit this experience, I feel, has changed me and even made me question what I am doing with these dogs, to create these extremely strong relationships with dogs that are not mine. I mentioned Blossom; she was an Outer Banks dog. Zeke was an Eastern Shore dog, and Pretty Girl and Scrappy are VB dogs.

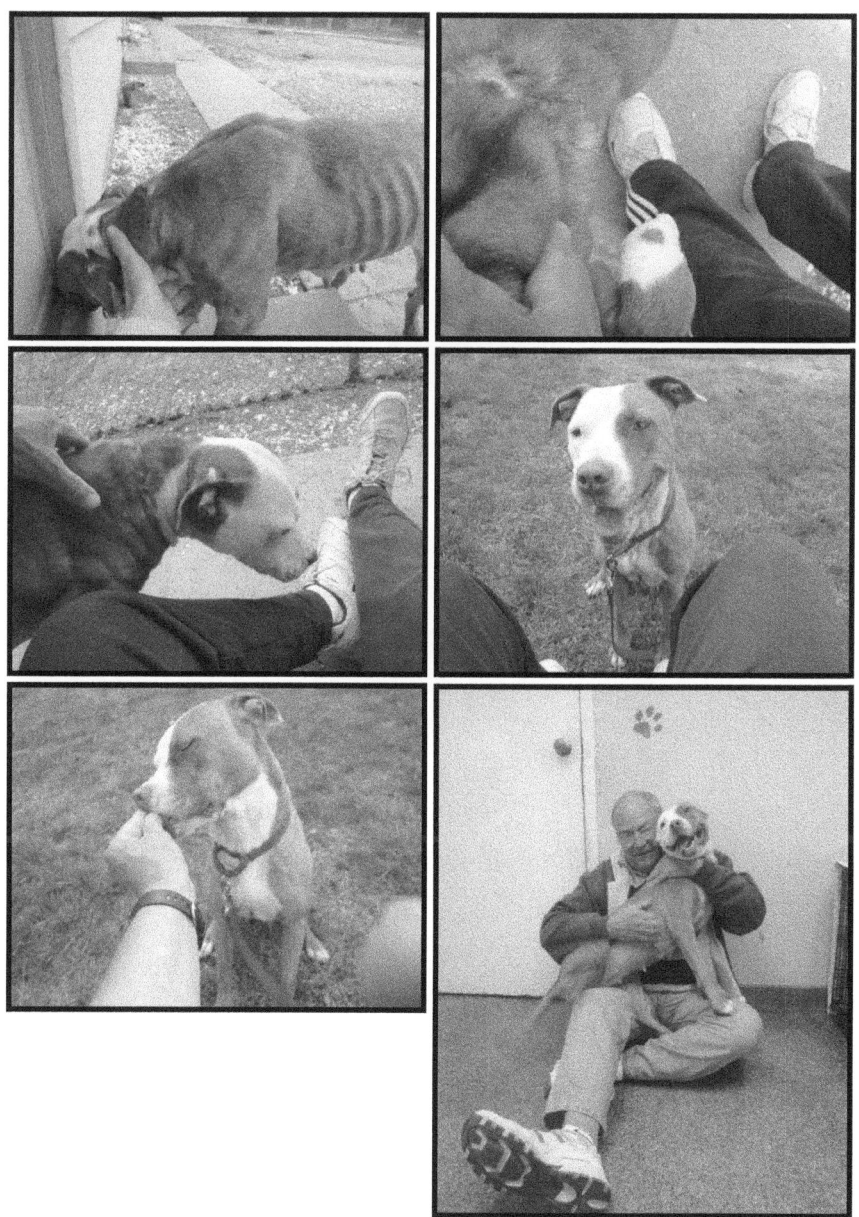

Chapter 6

Bo Duke

This is the story of a twelve-week-old Yellow Lab puppy that was surrendered to the Eastern Shore SPCA. At twelve weeks of age, he was on his third home, and it was an SPCA.

Bo Duke was originally owned by a young couple who didn't have a clue on what to expect when adopting a puppy. They quickly became overwhelmed and were very willing to hand him off to another young couple who showed an interest in him. Again, another young couple who didn't have any experience, and Bo Duke pretty much had his way with them and managed to get even further out of control.

I happened to be at the shelter when they "dumped" him off, just wanting to get out of a very bad situation. I met him that afternoon.

I can remember putting a leash on him and taking him outside to one of the fenced yards to get some time with him. I thought I had a horse on the other end of the lead! It was the closest thing to seeing a bucking bronco at a rodeo. He bucked and thrashed around like a wild horse. We tried to walk, but he constantly balked at being on a leash. The next day was more of the same, but we hung in there and continued with me just standing there and letting him jump around, but I remained unflappable.

We had an adoption event coming up, and my wife was going to walk him, but he proved to be a little too much with his antics. I continued to spend time with him being very firm but gentle. I started to see signs of progress with him standing alongside me. There would be moments that he would challenge me, but I would just stop moving, and he would soon settle down and was rewarded for his good behavior.

We went to the event, and I handled him, and he was really coming around at this point. People from the shelter saw his improvement and were quite surprised to see his progress.

While at the event, a young couple started to show some interest in him. I explained the circumstances and his background, and although the young man was not concerned, his wife did express some concern. I was a little worried because I didn't want to see a third failure for this very young puppy. I felt it could be very detrimental to this little guy to be abandoned again.

After some serious deliberation, the young couple took him. We discussed the leash issues, the positive reinforcement, and a very gentle demeanor and handling, and they took him.

All reports coming back were very positive. It appeared they were spending a lot of time with him, and things were going very well. We started getting pictures of him enjoying paddle boarding with his new owner, and when Christmas came, we received a picture of Bo Duke wearing Rudolph antlers.

He had a rocky start, but these young folks made the commitment and were going to stick by him unlike his past owners. They spent a lot of time with him and clearly gave him what he needed, love and positive reinforcement, and he responded beautifully. This success just reinforced my commitment to working with these misunderstood dogs and helping them find their forever home—a very rewarding effort!

Chapter 7

Blossom

Blossom came to the OBX SPCA as a stray. An individual showed up at the shelter, demanding a trap for a stray dog, or he claimed he would shoot her. The trap was issued, and he was told to call, and the dog would be picked up. One cold rainy morning, when the first shelter employee arrived at work, there was Blossom. She was soaking wet and trembling inside the trap, left at the entrance of the shelter.

My name is Jack Huh, I am a volunteer at the OBX SPCA, and she was there when I made my first visit to the shelter. The rest of this writing reflects my interaction with this wonderful dog for over a period of about several months.

The first day I saw her, I was not associated with the shelter. We had just purchased an OBX house, and I paid the shelter a visit just to look around. That was the first time I saw Blossom, and she was trembling in the corner of her kennel. Two weeks later, I went back and signed up as a volunteer and was quite surprised to see her still trembling in the corner of her kennel. I was immediately attracted to her and asked staff about her. I was told she was not aggressive, and staff put a leash on her, and I took her for a walk, outside the shelter. As we left the shelter, I remember thinking that she seemed almost in awe of the experience. I later learned, from a discussion with Debbie Jacobs, owner and author of the Fearful Dog website and a Fearful Dog book, that this dog was probably not physically abused, rather mentally abused. She was probably kept in isolation, with little or no human or canine contact. The outcome of such abuse will often produce a fearful animal.

Fearful animals can run in a range in this category, from fearful aggressive to fearful submissive. Having worked with my own fearful dog for over a year now, I have some understanding of the issues involved. My dog is fearful aggressive, and Blossom, in my opinion, is fearful submissive. In my time with her, I have never seen any aggression, to people or dogs, whatsoever. As a matter of fact, I would categorize her as a very sweet dog.

I continued to take her for walks, and we sat outside, getting to know each other a little better each time. Every trip started out the same way except now I leashed her and took her out. She continued to tremble in the corner when I entered her kennel and leashed her but stopped as we exited the kennel. I kept handling, to a minimum, with the early visits as she seemed uncomfortable with it.

We were advised by Debbie Jacobs that one of the first steps in rehabilitation is getting the dogs to take treats. Blossom was not taking treats, probably too scared to do so. We found that nuking small pieces of hot dog turned out to be something she eventually could not resist. I started tossing them to her, and that was how she started accepting them from me. We soon built the relationship to the point of taking treats from my hand.

With this accomplished, we now had the basics to begin a positive reinforcement for a behavior we were trying to introduce.

Her progress had been slow, but there was progress. She still trembled when I entered her kennel to get her, but that quickly dissipated. When we were out on walks, she looked up at me a lot. I have been told this positive behavior and should be rewarded.

In prior sessions, she would always keep her distance to the extent of a six-foot leash. She would now sit closer and allow me to place both hands on her and pet her for short periods. She would leave and return, allowing me to pet her.

To summarize, this is my opinion from my experiences with her. She is fearful submissive, now accepting treats, and now more tolerant of handling. She has never ever displayed any aggressive behavior during my visits with her. She will need owners with lots of patience to help her progress through this. Although we have made significant progress, she still has a long way to go. Ideally, the new owners will have some experience in this area. Fearfuldogs.com will help a potential owner get a better idea of what they will be dealing with.

When the shelter overcrowding issue became a reality, the Director called me and asked if my offer to move Blossom out was still an option, and of course it was. My plan was to board her somewhere until the crisis was over. The shelter was using RIAC for their vet needs, so that was where I went.

The details were worked out, and the next morning, one of the A/C folks delivered Blossom. I went there the next day to see her, and she was still guarded but seemed a little less frightened. This went on for a little while, and what I found out was that vet staff, mostly young women, were making a big fuss over her, and I could see the change beginning to happen with her.

When I noticed this, I went to the Director and explained the situation to her and asked if she would consider transferring Blossom's ownership over to the clinic. The answer was yes, so now I was off to the clinic. Dr. Burkart and I were in the lobby, and I was trying to find the right words to ask her for this very special favor. I remember being uncomfortable because I was concerned she would say no. As I struggled to find the right words, Dr. Burkart put an end to my awkwardness and said yes. The only condition was that the clinic would have complete ownership of her, so she could be adopted out of the clinic.

That was agreed to, and now Blossom had a new home. I would go there when I could and take Blossom for walks. Two young women behind the reception desk were talking about someone who would be a great foster mom for Blossom. I got an e-mail that they were going to move her to the foster to get her out of the clinic for the weekend.

I eventually got in touch with Tami, the foster mom, and she told me Blossom was doing well but still was a very troubled dog. Tami had two Pit mixes, which, in some cases, dogs can help with the rehab better than people.

I started to hear things like Blossom was sleeping in Tami's bed. One day I called Tami, and she started to say how hard it would be to give her up. I was quiet at first when she said that. I finally asked, "Are you going to adopt her?" Now Tami was quiet. She finally responded with a yes, and I could not have been happier.

Everyone was proud of her and happy for her. No matter what had happened to her in the past, she had made it.

I have helped save lives, and some at the eleventh hour, but this one has been the sweetest because of the living hell this wonderful dog had been through.

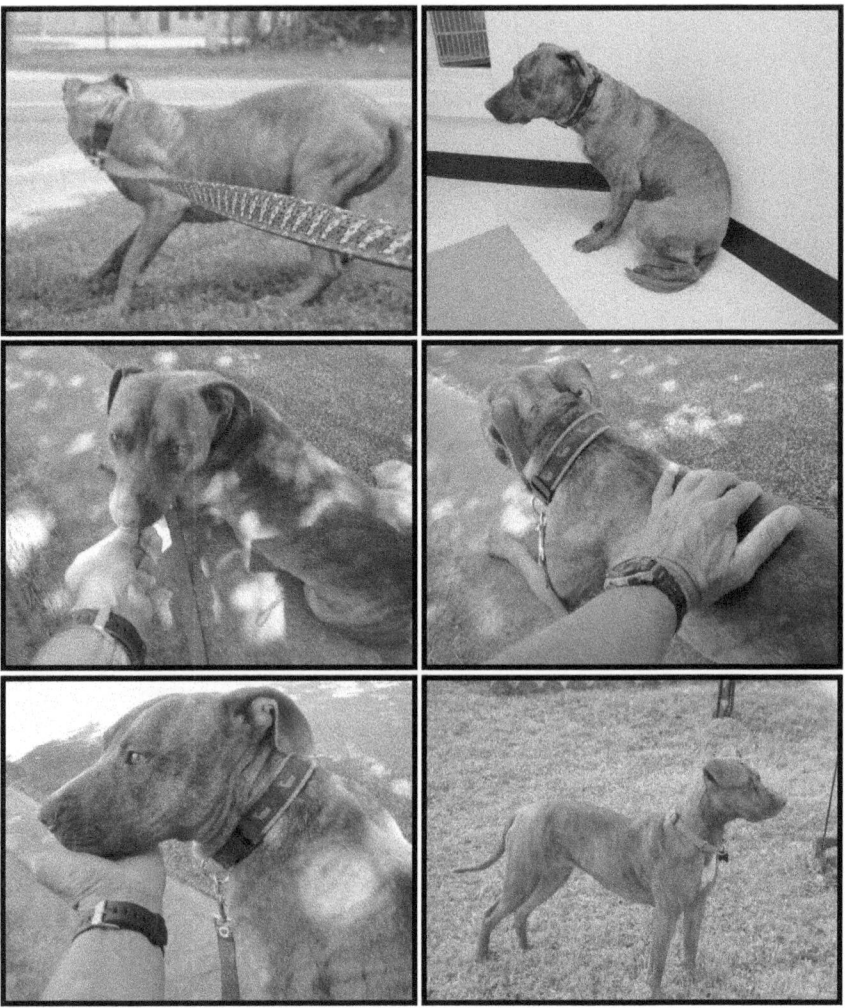

Chapter 8

Bella

Bella was one of two dogs owned by someone in the Outer Banks Frisco area. She was certainly not the favorite because she was an outside dog and allowed to just roam around. When this person moved, she took the other dog but left Bella behind to shift for herself. Our animal control was called, and she was picked up and brought to the shelter.

She was with us for a while, and as what happens with some of them, kennel life becomes quite difficult, and she began to have trouble coping. On one occasion, I took her for a ride, and my wife was along. We stopped somewhere, and I left the car to get something from a store. Bella became upset and very anxious with my departure but settled back down as soon as I got back into the car. It seems that some of these shelter dogs that are shown a little kindness can get very attached very quickly.

As we have found, sometimes a change of scenery will help, so shelter staff called RIAC, our vet, to see if they would help us out. If RIAC has the room, they will do it, but most of the time, they want to take ownership of the dog, and that was the case here. They do this so they can have control over the adoption process, and it works very well. Also, if we do something like this, we make it a habit of visiting the dogs frequently and get them out and work on socialization and obedience training. We stick with them until they find their new home.

I used to walk her around town with a ThunderShirt on her with the words "ADOPT ME" glued on the shirt. Several people called our SPCA, saying that some idiot was walking around town trying to peddle his dog. The SPCA responded by saying that everything was okay as the dog and the idiot belonged to them, the SPCA. So nice to feel wanted!

She had a couple of people interested in her, but conditions were not quite right like apartment living and so on. She is a big girl and needed space.

Eventually, the right couple came along, and she was very happily adopted, and she is doing very well.

Chapter 9

Lillie

Eastern Shore Animal Control on the Virginia Eastern Shore moves dogs to rescues every chance they get. The one area they run into problems with is moving Pits or Pit mixes. The local SPCA refuses pits, and most rescues are already filled with them. When space becomes an issue, they have no choice but to euthanize the longest kept dogs or dogs that they can't get adopted out. That means that Pits or Pit mixes may possibly end up being euthanized.

Recognizing that this situation existed, the Outer Banks SPCA agreed to try and help out, on a case-by-case basis, as long as they had room.

This story is about the first dog to be moved under this new agreement.

The agreement was that we would consider moving Pits or Pit mixes that appeared to be sweet dogs without any known issues. Although Eastern Shore A/C does not do temperament testing, they can get a feel for the dog's issues, especially if their stay becomes extended. On this visit, two dogs were selected as possible candidates for transfer. The first one that we looked at turned out to be in heat, so we put her back and looked at another one. Most of these dogs don't have names as they are strays. Both dogs seemed to be acceptable, but I was not sure if OBX wanted to deal with a dog in heat, so I checked and was told that was not an issue. I also found out that she had been a confiscated dog.

The owner had her tied outside without any shelter from the elements. He was warned twice, and when no corrective action was taken by the owner, the animal control officer confiscated her.

We made arrangements to take the dog in heat down to the OBX SPCA. I decided to name her Lillie and arrived at A/C about eight thirty the next morning to pick Lillie up. Stacey, an A/C staff member, leashed her, and we brought her outside for a potty break before bringing her over to the truck. I was going to reach down and pick her, but to our surprise, she jumped into the back seat and went right into the crate. I latched the crate door, closed the truck door, and Lillie and I were off for our three-hour-and-forty-five-minute drive to the Outer Banks SPCA. She behaved beautifully, and I never heard anything from her for the entire trip down.

When we arrived, I went in with the paperwork, and Kelsey, our kennel manager, came out to meet her and bring her into receiving. For about the next five or ten minutes, she was in Kelsey's arms, and both were loving every minute of their new friendship. Lillie's personality was surfacing, and she seemed to be so delighted to get the attention. More attention came from John, the Shelter Director, and Amy, a staff member. Lillie was loving every minute of all the attention she was getting. The next day, I went in and got her and gave her more attention. She absolutely was in heaven, loving every bit of the new fuss everyone was creating over her. We did notice a growl from her when she saw another dog on the other side of the fence, which raised a little concern. Also, that day, she had a visitor. A couple who volunteers and walks dogs spent some time with her and really enjoyed her, so much so that they decided to come back the next day to spend more time with her.

We decided that we would do an aggression assessment on her the next morning, Friday. Since she was in heat, we decided to do her last. We couldn't get her settled down and were never able to perform the first test, the "look" exercise. This is where you cup her face in your hands at look at her eyes and try and hold for three seconds. This is quite confrontational, and if there is aggression, it can show up here. Although we couldn't complete that part, there was no aggression in the attempt. All the rest of the tests went well with the last test being the dog to dog, with our stuffed dog named Rowdy. This was an area of concern as she had growled at a dog the previous day. When we brought

Rowdy out, Lillie charged Rowdy, and there appeared to be a little nip at Rowdy's ear, but Lillie lost interest and moved on. We gave her plenty of time on this test to make sure nothing else developed, but nothing did.

We brought her back to her kennel and met the couple who had spent time with her the day before. They were there looking for her and intended to spend more time with her, which we were grateful for. As for the rest of us, we had a team meeting scheduled, so it was back to business for us. When that was over, we broke up and did a few other things and had lunch. I decided to go back to the shelter and spend more time with Lillie, only to find out that she was gone. The couple who had expressed an interest in her decided to foster to adopt her and took her home. They were planning to get her spayed, and when I got home, there was an e-mail telling me how happy they were and sent pictures of her in her new bed.

I will have to say that I was quite overwhelmed by this whole experience. Not only was she a wonderful dog, but she had also found her family within a day and a half after spending six months in A/C with no one showing an interest in adopting her.

I do realize that this is still a foster to adopt, and it's not over yet, but it is sure looking good for Lillie. I also found out that her new owners live in the same neighborhood that we live in. We also have suggested that they bring her in for a couple of Thursday training sessions just to make sure things are going well.

An update to this is that Lillie was adopted by this couple and renamed Annabelle Lillie. They are absolutely delighted with her.

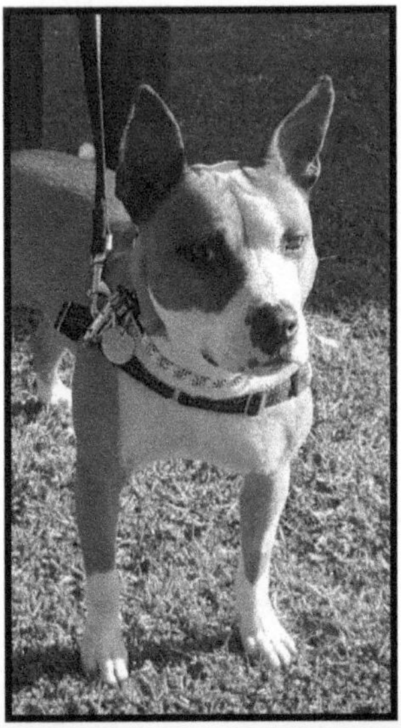

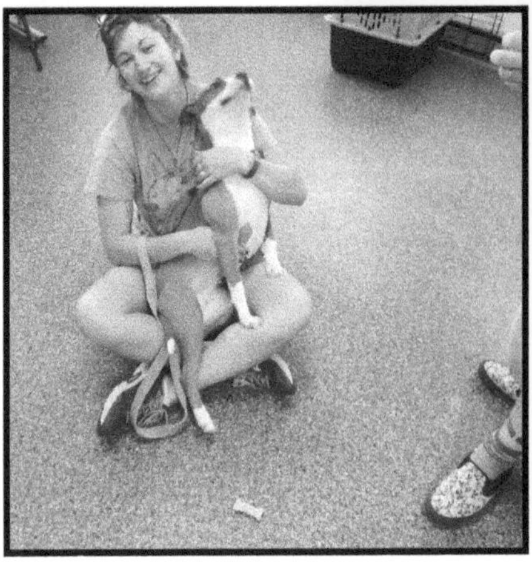

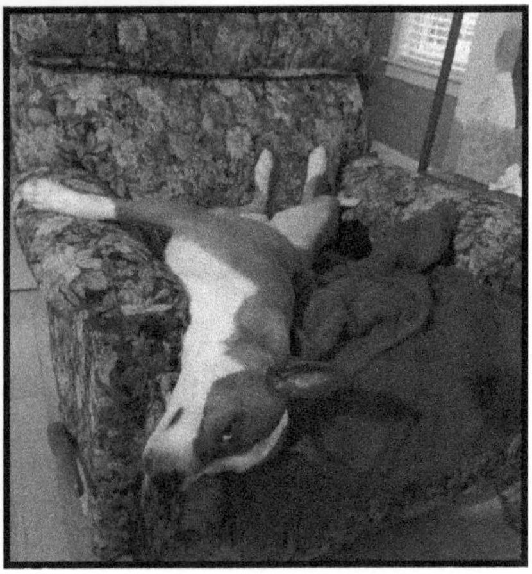

Chapter 10

Jessie

The Outer Banks SPCA and the Eastern Shore Animal Control facility have recently joined together in an effort to save the lives of Pit and Pit mixes that are either surrendered or picked up as strays on the Eastern Shore of Virginia. There is very little opportunity for these dogs to be re-homed on the Shore. The local SPCA refuses to handle anything with Pit in it, and rescues are generally full of them and not taking any more of them. The result is that these dogs end up by being euthanized for space issues.

The Eastern Shore Animal Control facility is a small facility with about twenty-eight kennels. By law, strays must be held eight days to allow for an owner to reclaim any lost dog. Many times, these are not lost dogs but rather dumped dogs or litters of puppies.

The arrangement to move these dogs is on a case-by-case basis and based on space availability at the Outer Banks facility.

The first move with Lillie was so successful we decided to bring number 2 down, another Pit mix that had been there since October, and again, it is March, and her time was getting short, and she really needed to be moved out. Again, early one Wednesday morning, a week after bringing Lillie down, I picked up a dog I named Jessie, and we left the Eastern Shore, headed for the Outer Banks.

Jessie was very good with other dogs and absolutely loved people. One of the animal control officers on the Eastern Shore spent some time with her and got her used to some rough handling, picking her and holding her upside down, and she loved the attention.

We had Jessie for about a week, had her spayed, and took her to an adoption event up in Duck. This event is usually attended by out-of-state people who are trying to "get away" for a few days and come to the Outer Banks. It is usually a two-day event, and Jessie was discovered on the first day of the event by some folks vacationing from Pennsylvania. They had gotten away without their children and were enjoying themselves for a few days. They happened to come across Jessie and were immediately taken by her. Also, by the way, she loved to play with children who would just come up to her. She would roll over for a belly rub. Jessie was in heaven, and she was showing it to everyone.

The rest of this story is documented below, and there are some priceless pictures to go along with it. Of particular interest is when Jessie was brought home to meet their two children and the circumstances around this adoption. See my communication with the adopting parents below.

Hi, folks, my name is Jack. We met today. I am the one who brought Jessie to the Outer Banks SPCA. She came from Melfa, Virginia, an animal control facility.

This facility has limited capacity, and although they are wonderful people who try very hard to place all the dogs, it just doesn't always happen. The dogs that are particularly affected by this are dogs that may even remotely look like they could have any Pit in them. Rescues are full of them, and there just isn't an outlet for as many as they take in. The result is they have to euthanize to make room for the new strays that, by law, must be kept a minimum of eight days. If space is needed, they start to euthanize if they are told to do so.

Your girl Jessie, as I named her, had been there since October and fell into the "must deal with" category. My wife and I have two homes, one in Virginia and the other in OBX. When we heard about the situation, thanks to management of both facilities, we were able to work out an arrangement where the Outer Banks SPCA would take, on a case-by-case basis, these dogs that were in trouble.

Jessie was the second dog brought down under this new arrangement. The first dog was brought down a week earlier and had been at that facility since September. She was adopted from our facility after being there only a day and a half. Jessie was with us for nine days.

So congratulations on finding her, and we know her life has been saved, and you, folks, have yourself a wonderful companion and family member. We are all delighted.

Please keep in touch with us and send pictures if you have the time to do so.

If this doesn't make you feel good, nothing will. Please remember, this dog was in trouble on the Eastern Shore. She had been in animal control since October and didn't even have a name. Her stay was just about over. Thanks to John and staff at A/C, an agreement has been worked out to take these in trouble dogs on a case-by-case basis. The point to be made here is she would have to be euthanized for space if she had to stay much longer.

We simply can't let this happen.

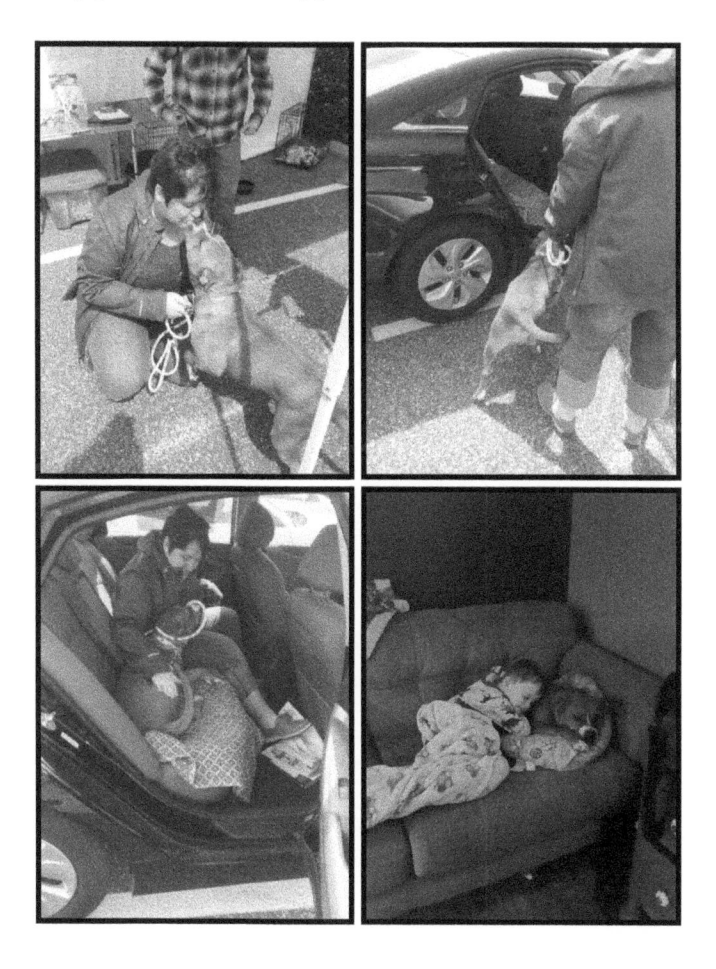

Chapter 11

Sky

I was contacted by Eastern Shore Regional Animal Control about a Pit Bull mix that had been surrendered and whose time was up. She needed to be moved for space. If no place could be found for her, she would be euthanized.

The dog belonged to a young person who got her and then went off to college. The mother didn't want the dog, so she surrendered her.

Sky was a beautiful dog, a little shy but had big fat cheeks that I couldn't keep my hands off. One day she was being walked by a volunteer, and she slipped out of her collar. She appeared to want to go into the shelter, but when she was approached, she took off. She was last seen heading down the side of a road and across a field.

After seeing her apparently wanting to get back in the shelter, it was decided to leave a gate at the back of the shelter property open as well as her kennel, and perhaps she would return on her own.

That was done, and the next morning, she was found in her kennel.

A family was visiting from out of state with a little girl, and they seemed to be very fond of her. After a couple of visits, they decided to adopt her. We have a great picture of mom, dad, and the little girl in the lobby with Sky just before they departed for home.

Everyone got lucky on this as Sky got a great home, and the family got a great little fat-cheeked dog, whom I was very fond of.

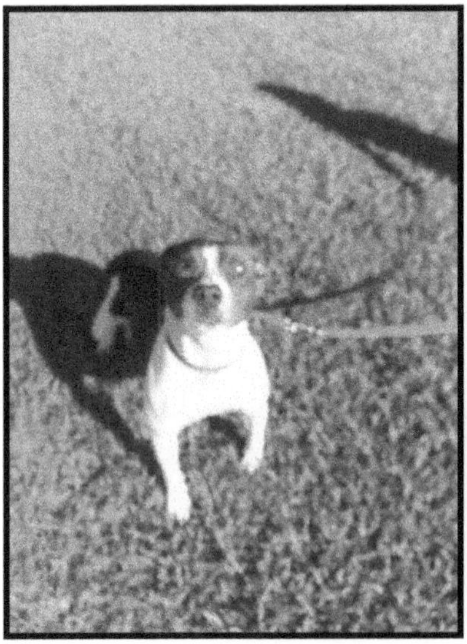

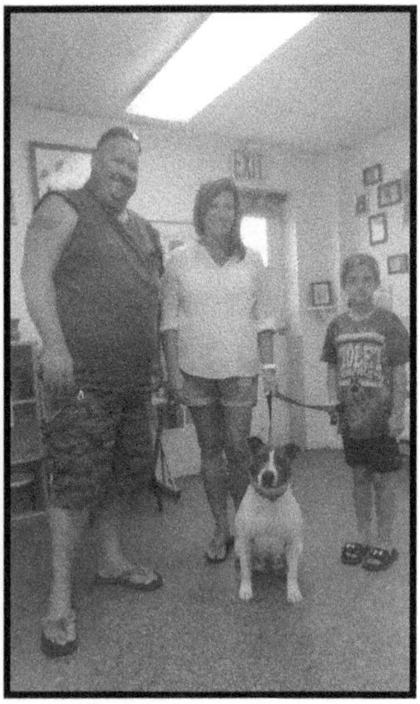

Chapter 12

Pretty Girl

Pretty Girl is an example of what can happen in a couple of hours between a shelter dog and a volunteer.

I was walking through the kennel at VB SPCA, and I noticed a dog lying on her kennel floor. As we all know, walking through a kennel creates a great deal of arousal, so when I saw a dog unresponsive, I knew something was wrong. I stopped and called her name, Pretty Girl, and got nothing from her. I went around to the back of the kennel, let myself in, and sat on the floor. There was no reaction from her at all. I called her name and offered a treat, still nothing. I remember thinking that I was looking at a dog that had given up. I could see hopelessness in her eyes.

I decided to go around to the front of the kennel, and I let myself in. She picked her head up and looked at me, and I slipped a leash on her, and we left the kennel and went outside.

When we got outside, I could see she was frightened, and I could feel the tension in her body. We remained outside for a short while, but it was clear she was uncomfortable, so I brought her inside, in hopes of finding a place where she would feel and become more relaxed.

I sat on the sofa in the lobby area, talking to her and petting her. I could still feel the tension and stiffness, but it was beginning to ease. She started to move around, and suddenly, she backed herself into a position between my knees. I continued talking and petting her, and she was calming down. A kennel staff member went by and commented that she had found a safe place, where she felt protected. Again, TRUST. She was starting to trust me. Who was this stranger that was suddenly providing a "safe place" for her, and what did it take to make this happen? I was talking to her, petting her, and, of course, had a very calm demeanor.

The assistant kennel manager had been watching this and came over to me and asked if she could take her from me. She told me she was going to be euthanized that day, and rather than return her to her kennel, it would be easier on her if it was done in this relaxed state. I was stunned and could not believe what I was hearing. I held on to the leash and asked for options. She said that someone showed an interest, but as happens so often, they never came back. VB has a policy that when the perceived condition of the dog is so miserable, it is better to humanely end that life rather than let the suffering continue. The decision is also done by a committee. I understand that logic to some degree, but who is to say that the next person who walks through that door is not going to be the person who will provide the forever home for the dog?

I finally turned over the leash and left. Needless to say, my emotional state was not very good. I had an hour-and-a-half ride home to think about it. My phone started to ring, but I was in no condition to answer it. Whoever it was kept calling, and I was about to shut it off when I noticed it was my wife. She told me the shelter was trying to reach me to tell me something had been worked out, and they were trying to reach me to give me the details. They contacted the people who expressed an interest and found out because of some personal issues, they had to delay picking her up but would be there for her in the morning.

The "trust" word came up again. In two hours, this dog went from a hopeless state to responding to the human touch and kindness. What made me go there that day? What made me find her and go to her? How did these two individuals, canine and human, connect with each other? I don't know any of the answers to these questions, but I seemed to be driven by a gut feel. Imagine if that didn't happen.

The experience of holding a trembling dog and bringing it to a calm state is something not easily forgotten. I have had that experience with my own hoarder dog named Scrappy, Blossom, this one, and a few others. Under the old way of thinking and dog training, it was believed that doing this was encouraging or rewarding this type of behavior. Times have changed, and thinking has also changed.

If anyone would like to learn more about this, you can visit www.fearfuldog.com. Debbie Jacobs is the owner of the website and the author of an e-book by the same name. She helped me work through issues with my Scrappy and gave advice on Blossom, an OBX shelter dog. She discussed this safe place with me as well. I took a small dog crate, took the door off, put some pillows in it, and covered it with a blanket. Scrappy can push past the blanket to enter, and once inside, he is able to push the pillow in a way that the opening is fully closed. You cannot tell he is in there. This is his safe place, and he goes in there when he feels he needs to. We have one at each house, and he nested both to get them the way he wants them.

Obedience training, exercise, agility training, socialization, and behavior modification and enrichment are all part of the package shelter dogs need. Sometimes some need a little more. Sometimes they need to be held, comforted, and be able to feel they can trust again. These are very special dogs, on the road to recovery.

A while back, I spent an hour with a dog at the shelter that was not trembling but wanted to be held so badly. He is a big boy but wanted to be in my lap so badly I had to let him. I also brushed him at the same time, and he seemed like he was in heaven. His name is Otis.

I have seen many shelter dogs that seem well adjusted with a happy-go-lucky personality that in their present state don't really need this extra touch, at least not currently. It's the Blossoms, the Pretty Girls, and the Scrappies that do need it.

Attached is a picture of a safe place.

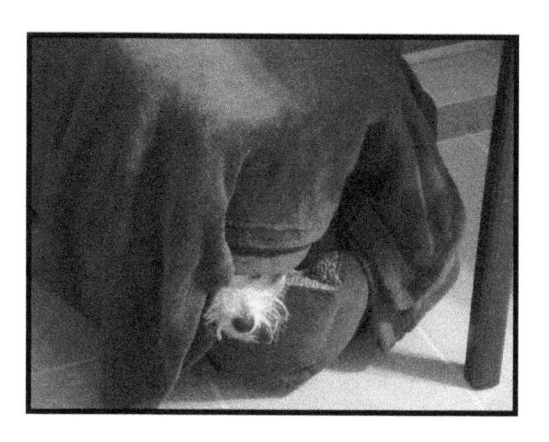

Chapter 13

Longshot

On one of my trips to the Eastern Shore Animal Hospital, I was told about a Yellow Lab that was found on the side of the road, in a roadside ditch, that had been shot. Evidentially, someone had shot him with a shotgun, hitting him in the right shoulder and head area. He was found and immediately transported to the Eastern Shore Animal Hospital. He was cleaned up, hair shaved off in the direct hit area, and evaluated to determine his possible chances of survival.

Apparently, he was shot from a distance because the shot didn't reach any internal organs. Speculation is that someone saw him and deliberately tried to kill him, or perhaps someone was poaching and heard or saw something moving in the bushes and took the shot, only to find they had shot a dog. Either way, he was left in the woods to die.

Labs have amazing resiliency, and he managed to crawl to the roadside ditch, where he was found. After evaluation, it was determined that he had a chance of survival but could possibly have to lose an eye, but he was alive.

Time went by, and he started to heal well, but it became apparent that the eye was causing discomfort and needed to be removed.

I met up with him during his recovery and was told about how he refused to get into a vehicle, probably some association with an unpleasant past experience. We used Dr. Paula's car and worked on luring him into the car. It worked beautifully. I could get him to jump into the back seat and also into the tailgate area. When we first started to work on this, he would resist by just pancaking on the ground. He would just lie flat on the ground and refuse to stand. He must have practiced this because he was quite good at it.

By now, he had healed up quite well, including his eye, and after discussing with hospital staff, it was decided he would be moved to the OBX SPCA for training and possible adoption. What was learned about him, while he was staying at the hospital, was that he was an escape artist and could climb a chain-link fence. He was caught a couple of times, and one time, in back-to-back fenced yards, he decided to join the dog in the adjoining yard. Imagine the surprise of staff when they put the dogs in separate yards and checked on them to find them in the same yard. OBX SPCA was well aware of his escape tendencies, and he was kept in a covered inside yard that if he did get out of, he would still be contained within the facility.

As time went on at OBX, volunteers started spending time with him, and his training continued. We worked on basis obedience training and also training to not have him bolt through an open door. He was doing very well.

One day a person who was on OBX for vacation decided to do a shelter walk through and saw him in the kennel. They inquired about him and were told of his history. The person turned out to be a blogger for the *Huffington Post* and decided to write up the article as they thought they understood it, which was actually incorrect. It was titled something like from "Famous to Pound." It implied that the hospital dump him on us.

When the hospital heard about it, they called me and asked me to bring him back home to them. Of course, we complied with their request as he really was their dog. So early one morning, Longshot and I got loaded up and got ready to leave OBX. As we were about to leave, some guy came up and asked if he could see Longshot as he had heard the story about him. All he wanted to do was see him for himself so he could confirm that, in fact, there really was a Longshot because the story seemed so bizarre.

After a few moments of discussion, Longshot and I departed on the three-and-a-half-hour trip back to the animal hospital on the Virginia Eastern Shore.

I didn't realize it at the time, but the local press was at the hospital and wanted to interview the hospital staff and myself as to what had happened and what the future plans were for him. It went well, but it was apparent that there were no real plans for his future yet. It would just be a wait-and-see situation looking for the right adopter, which eventually did happen. A couple with another Yellow Lab visited and were definitely interested. After several meetings, the decision was made to let him go.

Everything has ended well for him. His wandering days seem to be behind him as he is very content with his new mom, dad, and brother. He is left off leash and just stays home, a happy ending to a very rough start for this beautiful and amazing dog.

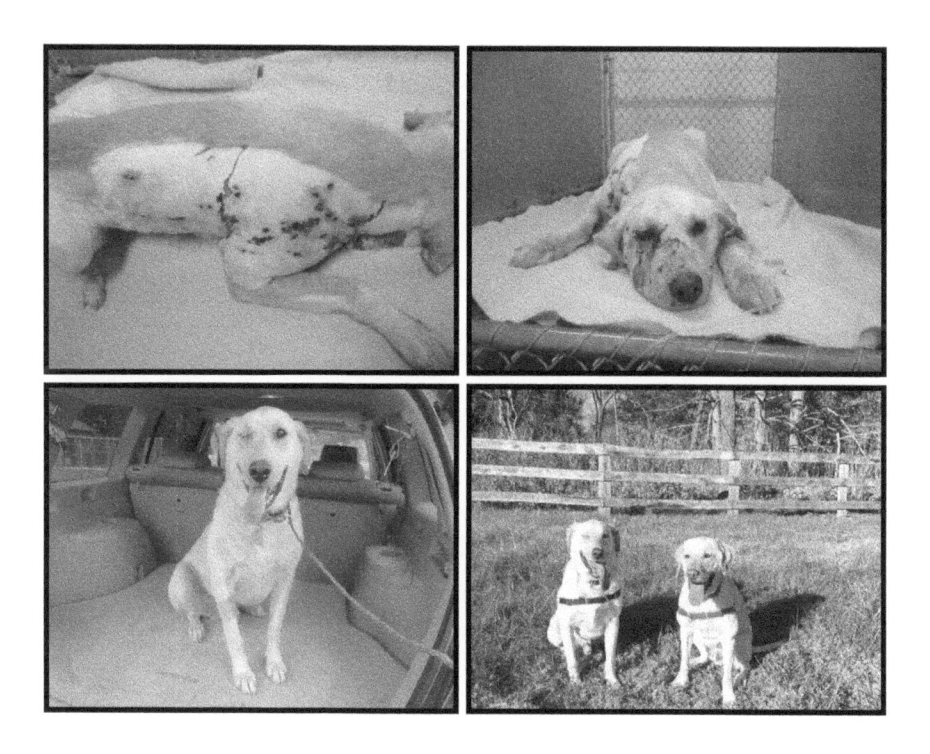

Chapter 14

Lucas

Lucas is an Eastern Shore of Virginia dog that was found in an emaciated condition and brought to the Eastern Shore Animal Hospital. He was nursed back to health, including getting neutered and cured for heartworm. All his medical treatment was complementary of the Eastern Shore Animal Hospital.

When he was healthy enough, he was transferred to the Outer Banks SPCA, where he would hopefully be adopted.

As it turns out, Lucas had difficulty handling kennel life. He became mouthy and caused a previous cut on a volunteer's hand to reopen, causing minor bleeding.

He was returned to the Eastern Shore Animal Hospital while we looked for adoption options and later transferred to an SPCA in Delaware.

I have personally spent a lot of time with him and feel he is a great dog that needs a chance.

The Christmas morning of 2016, I received an e-mail that Lucas was adopted. My prayers for this wonderful dog have been answered. He really should be my dog, but three dogs are just too much for us.

What a wonderful Christmas present this is to know that he is safe and will be loved.

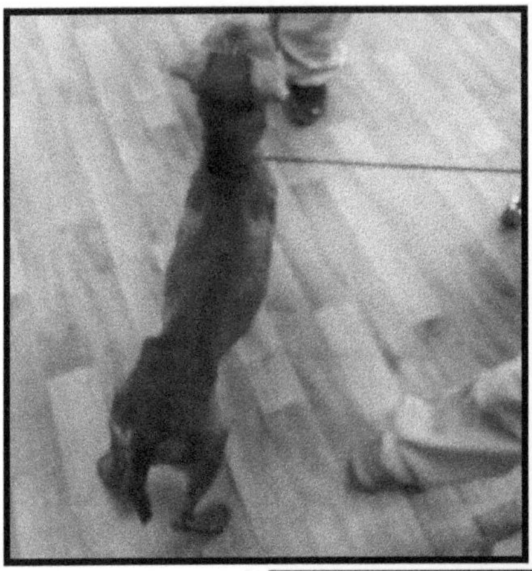

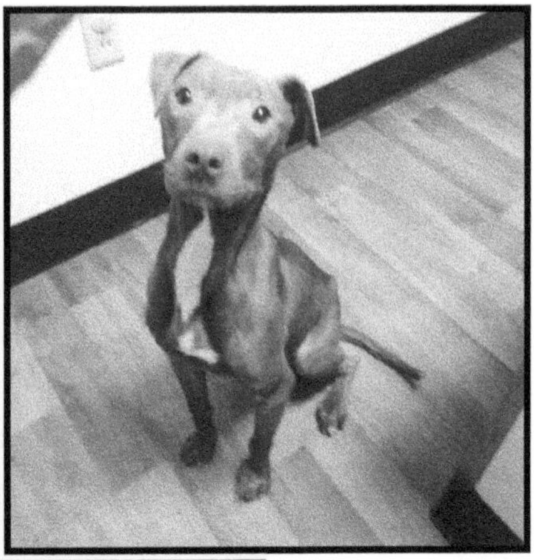

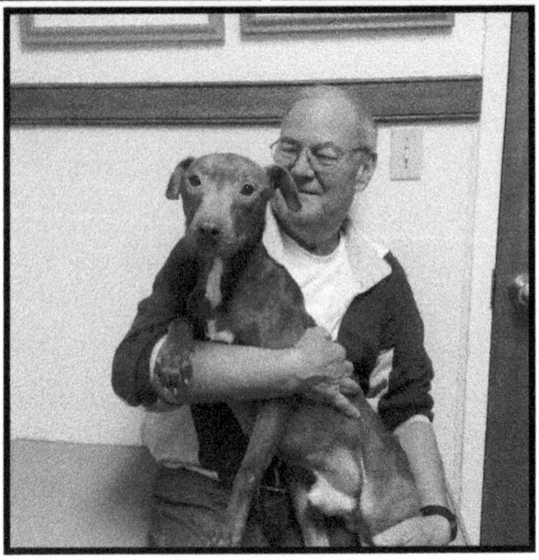

Chapter 15

Patches

I was contacted by Britney of the Eastern Shore Animal Hospital about a dog that had been dumped off on the dead-end street where her parents live. They had taken her in, but she was on an outside run. She felt they needed help finding her a home, so I was contacted.

After seeing pictures, I got permission to relocate her to the Outer Banks SPCA.

She was a very good girl on the trip down, and when checked into receiving, things went very well. She was bathed, and all the rest of the receiving tasks were taken care of.

She was not spayed, and that was taken care of within a day of her admission. There was a sense of urgency because there was an event on Saturday that we wanted her to attend.

The event was great, and she got a lot of attention. Most notable was the relationship between Patches, as I named her, and a volunteer named Dez. Patches found Dez's lap and remained there for most of the duration of the event. Dez was falling in love as it was very easy to do.

She was brought back to the shelter and went out on foster. Stacey already had a dog but is a working single mom, so Patches was left home. This was when we found out that she had separation anxiety. She somehow managed to get out of her crate and did a lot of chewing in the house. She even chewed on a door to get to play with the resident dog that was behind the door. I went and picked her up and brought her back to the shelter.

Within a couple of days, she went out on foster again, this time to a home with two Pugs and people who were retired. There was no separation anxiety, but one of the Pugs had a jealously issue, and there was a cat issue, so Patches was brought back to the shelter.

Dez, the woman who handled her at the event, took her out on foster. This was a very good environment for Patches, and she thrived. Dez had two other dogs and two cats. The dogs played together, and the cats were not an issue. Dez also had an eleven-month-old baby, which also was also not an issue. Dez soon realized, as much as she loved Patches, that three dogs and two cats were a little much. With Thanksgiving and some adoption events coming up, she brought Patches back to the shelter to have a chance at an adoption.

Dez had great instinct on this as shortly after Dez's departure from the shelter, a woman came in looking for a companion for her dog and was drawn to Patches. To ensure she was fully informed about what we knew about Patches, John spent time with her, going over all the e-mails he had on her. The real only negative was the separation anxiety. After the discussion was over, Patches left for her new home. I believe the new owner had two homes, with one being on the Outer Banks.

We are very happy for Patches because it looks like this time conditions are right, and she has found her new home. She is an extremely lovable dog, and we are sure all will be very happy.

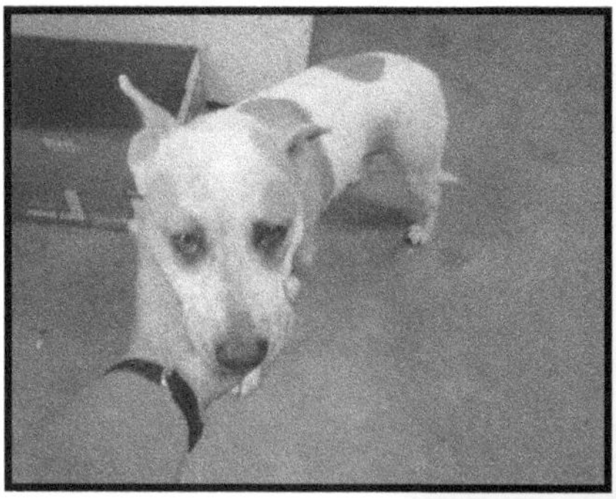

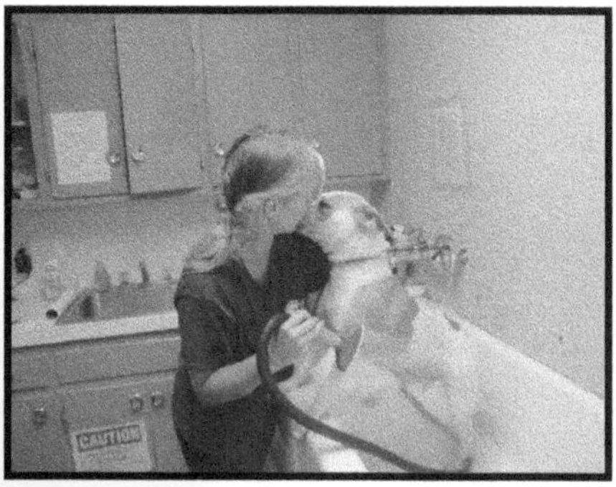
CAUTION

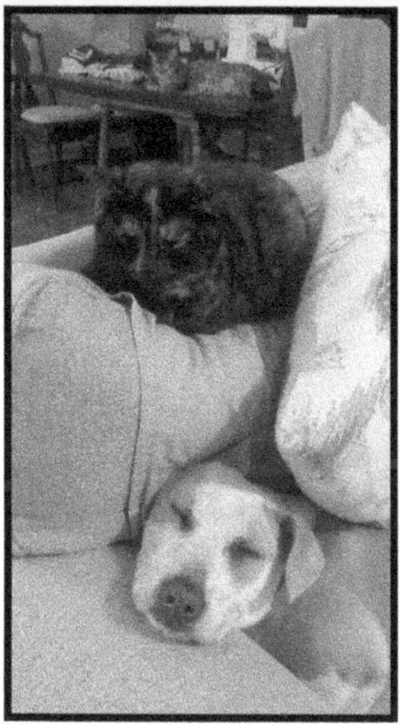

Chapter 16

Sammy

This is the story about the dog that its owner surrendered him to the OBX SPCA with specific instructions that he be euthanized. After the dog was surrendered and belonged to the shelter, he was looked at, and there didn't seem to be an apparent reason to take his life. One of the staff members, who would have had to do the euthanasia, refused to do it.

A rescue was called, and I was called and asked if I would be willing to transport a dog to a rescue. When the details were explained, I agreed, and very early the next morning, Sammy and I left the Outer Banks and headed to meet the rescue at the North Carolina–Virginia border.

I didn't get to spend much time with him but enough to be at a loss for the decision to euthanize him. He was very calm and a very sweet dog. The transfer was made, and within a week, we received news that he had been placed in a very good home, and some pictures followed.

I really give credit to the staff member for saving this dog's life. Sometimes you face things that are just plain wrong, and this was one of those times. I was proud to be part of the effort to save this guy's life.

less strain in facial muscles, and ears in a forward position instead of back and sideways.

Another exercise we worked on was letting me get between her and her safe place. With her being in the interior kennel, I would advance my physical position in the exterior kennel to the halfway point, and she would cross over me, placing me between her and her safe place, or the interior kennel. She was starting to trust me. Also, with this came more eating out of my hands.

A young woman visited the shelter, and she owned a Jindo dog, which is what Bailey was. She easily could connect with Bailey and decided to foster her. I was delighted to hear the news but also felt a little disappointed that I didn't have more time with her. As it turns out, Bailey was adopted by this young family and fit right in with the other dogs and even a cat.

Time went by, and I was sent a Facebook link about a Korean dog running away from home and traveling from Kill Devil Hills up to Corolla, North Carolina. There were pictures of her attached, and I recognized her as Bailey. My heart sunk, knowing what this dog had already been through, so I headed up to Corolla to start and search for her. I was driving around roads in Corolla Light, stopping people as they were walking, asking if they had seen a white medium-sized dog that resembled a German Shepherd. I finally came across a mom and daughter who had seen her, and I gave them Aubrey's phone number for them to call her. The information they gave was that she was seen on the beach, but she was headed south. We later got some conflicting information that she was seen on the four-wheel drive beach, north of Corolla.

Shortly after this, we received information that she had been spotted on the beach in Nags Head. I happened to be in the area of Nags Head that day, so I headed down to mile marker 20 or 21. I started to walk the beach, giving Bailey's description to everyone I could on the beach. I told them to call the SPCA if they saw her. One woman asked me for my phone number, which I gave to her. Her name was Norma, and she was staying at one of the beach houses at marker 21. She started asking people also and came across an older couple, with two small dogs, who claimed they were feeding Bailey. She called me, and I picked her up, and we raced over there. While we were talking with them, I looked over their shoulder, and I couldn't believe there was Bailey. I called her, and she started to go the other way. I followed her in my jeep, and she made a left on a dead-end road that ended on the beach. I called her again, and she started to run. I realized at this point that she would not come to me. I felt I was just making matters worse, so I abandoned my pursuit of her and just notified the owner of what happened.

I gave Aubrey the names and phone numbers of the people who had seen her and just prayed for the best.

Aubrey and her husband had a trap, but it was set up in Corolla. He was working at the time, but the plan was to pick up the trap and head down to Nags Head, set up the trap where she was being fed, and sleep on the beach that night.

So the plan was established and implemented, and at six o'clock the next morning, I received a text with hearts and doggie footprints. I tend to be emotional when it comes to working with shelter dogs, and this was about as good as it gets.

We had a similar experience with our rescue dog, running away for three weeks on the Eastern Shore of Virginia, so we could really relate to this and the emotions felt by Aubrey and her husband. Getting our little boy back was a moment we will never forget, and this was the same.

The thing to realize about this is that there were many people involved, all wanting the best for Bailey and owners. Another point is that Aubrey took the position that it was going to happen, not if it would happen but just when it would happen.

THE POWER OF POSITIVE THINKING!

So now Bailey is reunited with family, and all has ended well. Maybe a gray hair or two for the owners, but Bailey is safe.

Chapter 18

Lola

Around the beginning of January 2018, I heard of a couple of dogs that had been rescued by Dune Dawgs Rescue, owned and operated by Henni Rains, that were being boarded at Hatteras Island Pet Resort in Rodanthe.

I stopped in one day and met the owner of the facility, Katie Greutman, and introduced myself and explained how I worked with shelter dogs, and my true love was working with abused and fearful dogs. We discussed a dog named Lola that was currently there and the fact that there was another Dune Dawgs rescue named Rosa that was currently out on foster.

I spent a few brief moments with Lola, but it was long enough to see she was a magnificent dog and had great potential for the kind of work I do. I was convinced that despite the abuse she had seen, she loved people and would be a lap dog.

I asked about seeing her on a regular basis, and there didn't seem to be any reason as to why not do so.

I decided not to use treats with her as I felt they were not necessary. My observation was that the motivation was already there to be with people and handled by people, and I was correct.

I started sitting on the floor with her, and she very quickly found her way to my lap. I was able to pet her, give her back rubs, and scratch her neck, and she was loving them.

I soon received some pictures of Lola shortly after she had been rescued. She was a bag of bones, and she was heartworm positive.

A week or so after first meeting her, she went for her last heartworm shot. She had also been at the Pet Resort for some time now and had put on weight and filled out beautifully.

We have had numerous visits now, and she is very content sitting close to me and being handled. She has her self-confidence back as she holds her head high and has lost that look of helplessness that she had in her eyes. She no longer has to worry about where and when she will eat again and what abuse will come next.

Her body language has changed, along with her facial expression, how she carries herself, and the look in her eyes.

We don't know what the future holds for Lola, but ideally, she will find a loving permanent home or a foster that will lead to that as she certainly deserves the best she can get; she has more than paid the price with abuse.

I will continue to spend time with her and enjoy her, even though she can't be mine.

An update, she is in foster to adopt.

Chapter 19

Lyla

I was introduced to Lyla on assessment day. We were told that she came from an abusive home and didn't like men, so it was decided Melissa would do the assessment.

She scored twos and threes on the assessment, and it was clear that she was very uncomfortable with the process.

We found out that she was owned by a young man who had moved and left her behind with his mother. The mother remarried, and the new husband soon became abusive to the wife and the dog in the house. The dog was pulled from the house by Dune Dawg Rescue and brought to the OBX SPCA, where I met her.

I was asked to see if I could help her adjust and see about improving the gender issue.

Below is an account of the days Lyla and I spent together.

Day 1

I spent some time with Lyla today. She was easily approachable and ate out of my hand, almost immediately. I guess tiny cut-up pieces of hot dogs are hard to pass up.

I let myself into her kennel and sat on the floor. I hadn't planned on hands on, but the opportunity presented itself, so I took it, and she allowed it.

She was very preoccupied with what was going on outside the kennel as John was doing play groups. It was very hard to keep her focused. I will visit her again tomorrow and see if things change tomorrow. There were no signs of aggression or discomfort with me handling her. She never turned her head in the direction of my hands or pulled away. I have not won her over yet, but it was a good start. I don't see her being a lap dog, at least not yet!

Attached are some pictures of the process.

Day 2

I let myself into her kennel, and she was a little aroused, but I quickly had her taking treats from my hand, and things were going well. She would sit and give her paw in return for treats.

Suddenly, it was like something set her off, and she retreated to her inside kennel, barking. She looked at me from her inside kennel and continued to bark at me. Her eyes were no longer soft.

I tossed some treats on the floor in an attempt to get her back with me, which worked, but she continued to look at me and bark.

I extended my cupped hand, full of treats, which she ate from but looked at me and continued to bark at me. This went on with taking the treats, looking directly at me, and continuing barking. I did not hold eye contact.

I fed her the rest of the treats from my hand, and when she retreated to her inside kennel, I let myself out.

She did not allow hands on today, and although it started out okay, she was clearly acting differently than yesterday.

I can't think of anything that could have caused the change in her, and I will be back with her tomorrow.

Day 3

Much better day today! I went there, and she was in a play yard. I let myself in and sat on the bench. I was loaded with chicken breast, hot dogs, and cut-up string cheese. There was no barking today, although she was a little preoccupied with the dog in another play yard. She ate from my hand and allowed some touching but would pull away after a short while.

Her eyes were softer today, and at one point, I caught her with her eyes closed. I might have caught that in the pictures I will attach.

She doesn't seem interested in developing a relationship; it's more of a what can you do for me now type of situation.

I will have to say that this is new for me, but maybe I am doing better than I think because I hear she doesn't like Paul. I have heard that twice now.

Anyway, my plan is to keep spending time with her as I would love to see some affection from her but doubt that will happen.

Those of you remember Max growling and showing teeth to staff and suddenly kissing everyone in sight. I don't see that happening here, but there is absolutely no aggression.

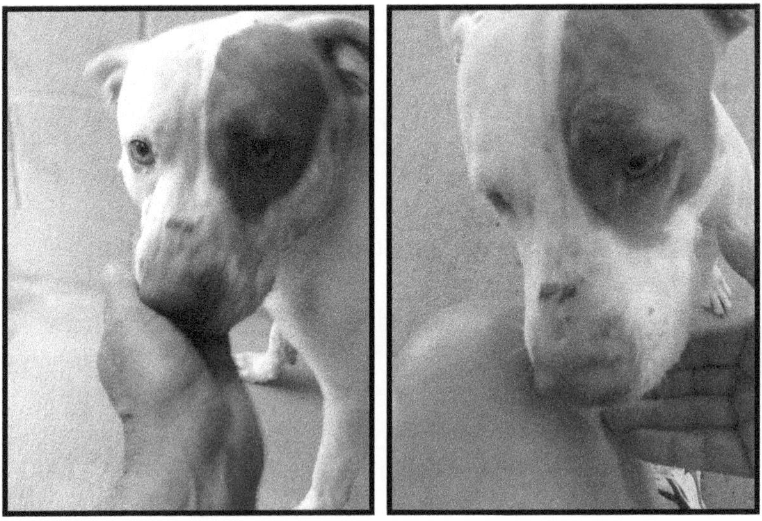

Chapter 20

Max

I was asked by the Shelter Director of the Outer Banks SPCA if I would consider working with a fearful dog that had just been surrendered.

Working with fearful dogs is something that I love doing as watching the transformation can be absolutely an incredible experience. This one was no exception and perhaps one of the most enjoyable of all since it happened in only six days. By contrast, I have spent as long as sixty days with a dog and not have been as successful as I was with this one. Much of this depends on how badly traumatized or abused the dog has been.

The following is an accounting of those six days. Each day was documented, along with photos of most of those days. The facts surrounding her, prior to being admitted to the shelter, are a little foggy, but here is what I have been told.

Her family was moving and, for whatever reason, couldn't take her. A neighbor found out that she was surrendered and came in and took her on a foster. She was returned after a couple of weeks because of some house training issues and getting out of a crate.

Upon her return, she was very frightened, and staff was unable to handle her without her growling and baring her teeth. Frightened dogs may protect themselves anyway they know how if they feel they are in danger. I have worked with fearful submissive as well as fearful aggressive dogs, Blossom being fearful submissive and my Scrappy being fearful aggressive. He bit five people and was to be euthanized, but instead, he is now our dog.

Here is Max's story, starting with the first day I started working with her.

Day 1

Today I had a chance to visit Max, the fearful dog that John asked me to spend time with. She is absolutely beautiful, and if I was looking for a dog, I would adopt her.

She was moved back into isolation because she was so frightened. She stays in the indoor kennel, but there was evidence that she relieved herself in the outside kennel, so maybe she is house-trained. I sat on the floor, outside of her kennel. and tossed some cut-up hot dogs her way. and I was ignored. She clearly was frightened. I talked to her for a while, and she seemed to calm down a little and sniffed a piece of hot dog that had landed right under her nose. She ate it and then another. I put some in the palm of my hand, and to my surprise, she started to eat out of my hand. Handful after handful until two hot dogs cut up into tiny pieces were gone!

She is clearly fearful in the shelter surrounding but responds beautifully to a little kindness and at her speed. Pushing it would probably only cause regression.

Her being in iso helps to keep her in a quieter environment and makes it easier for me to make progress with her. I will spend time with her every day, again at her pace.

Day 2

Today when I went there, I found her in the outside kennel. Normally dogs like this will retreat to the safety of their indoor kennel when approached, but she remained in the outside kennel. I knelt down and started to talk to her, and she growled at me. I dropped some cut-up hot dogs through the fence, and she quickly ate them.

I opened the kennel door and dropped some more pieces of hot dog on the floor, and she quickly ate them also. I put more in the palm of my hand and offered them to her, and she ate all of them from my hand. This went on for a while with the kennel door open even more.

Her eyes softened, going from wide-eyed to almond-shaped, as she continued to eat from my hand. At one point, I cupped her muzzle in the palm of my hand, and she was perfectly content with me doing so.

We finished up the hot dogs, and I said goodbye to her until tomorrow.

This beautiful little girl has had her world turned upside down, and she is struggling to understand what is going on as she is a surrender.

My intention is to be with her every day and take baby steps to win her trust. I believe she could be a lap dog under the right circumstances.

Day 3

Today when I got there, she was in the inside kennel. I let myself into the outside kennel and sat on the floor. I called her name and was ignored. I tossed some pieces of hot dog close to the divider wall but in the outside kennel, hoping that would be enough to get her to come out, but she wouldn't budge.

I tossed some to her in the inside kennel, which she ate, and that was enough to make her move to the outside kennel and eat the ones close to the divider wall. I tossed a few more, closer to me, which she also took, and then put some in the palm of my hand, and she came to me and ate them. I felt comfortable enough to touch her cheek and then the side of her neck and give her more treats. At this point, I put the camera down and had both hands on her. There was a little lip licking, but soon, she seemed to become very relaxed and started to close her eyes. I was able to pet her head, back, and shoulders. Never once did she pull away, try to leave, or show any discomfort or aggression.

I also tried to see if I could get between her and her safe place, the inside kennel. I did this with Bailey, the fearful Korean dog, and it took a while to accomplish this, but with Max, it was quite easy. Bailey kept going back and forth between the inside kennel and outside kennel as she was not trusting what was going on but not so with Max. She was very comfortable with me getting between her and her safe place.

I will probably stay with this for a while and then maybe introduce a collar and work on taking it on and off. I used to do that with Zeus, and he would allow me to put it on him and take it off him.

This is very similar to what I went through with Scrappy at the VB SPCA. I got a call from the shelter manager on the fourteen hoarder dogs that had just come in. Because of the distance, I would only go in a few times a week. I was spending a lot of time with Scrappy because he was biting people that tried to pick him up. I would just sit in his kennel with him, and one day he climbed on my lap and curled up and stayed there. It's all about trust!

This is a very sweet dog, and I would really like to take her, but I have two major obstacles, Scrappy and Charlene.

Day 4

My intention was to spend time with Max, but I was not going to send anything out on it because I really didn't expect anything new to happen, but I was wrong. She quickly came out from the inside kennel and was rewarded with tiny pieces of hot dog. She normally licks my hands because they are covered with hot dog residue. This time she licked my arms as well and allowed a lot of petting. I looked at her and noticed she had her eyes closed a lot of the time when I was petting her.

The other thing new was that she was content to curl up right by me and lie on the floor with her body touching me. She is absolutely melting me! I can feel the trust as I handle her. She is no longer tense. This has gotten way out of hand. My wish is that she will go to someone that I know so I can stay in her life as I have with a couple of others. I have learned that they don't forget you. I visited one dog, and he crawled under my truck and wouldn't come out. I had pulled him right before he was to be euthanized and boarded him until I found a home for him.

Day 5

Today she seemed a little nervous. She still ate from my hands and let me pet her, which I did plenty of, but there was some trembling, and she went inside and outside a couple of times. She also seemed to listen to what was going on in the kennel, which is something new.

She did sit very close to me but did not push up against or lean on me as she did yesterday. Also, her eyes remained open today as opposed to yesterday, where she seemed to be so at peace with everything by closing her eyes. We did make direct eye contact numerous times, but I didn't hold it, rather continued to pet her, which she allowed.

Maybe the weather had her a little spooked. I have one dog that could care less about the weather and another that will head for his safe place and not eat sometimes because of bad weather moving in. We are continuing to learn more about her.

I was told today by staff that she keeps a clean indoor kennel.

Day 6

I had decided that we were at a point with Max that we need to get more people involved with her, so I called for help from Melissa Kahn, our dog behaviorist. It was decided we would meet with her the next afternoon and see what else we could introduce to her.

I got there early and cut up the hot dogs and went back into her kennel. Shortly after doing so, I was joined by Abby, Melissa, and Lisa. It was decided that we would leash her, and all go to a play yard. Not knowing what to expect, I put the leash on her, and everything went well, and Abby took her, and we all proceeded to the yard. She was turned loose, and we just waited to see what would happen next. No one tried to touch her, this was at her speed, and I was truly amazed at what happened next. Everyone was sitting on the ground except for me as I was manning the camera. First, it was Lisa's turn as Max climbed on her and allowed petting. After that came Melissa. Melissa was sitting on the ground, and Max climbed on her, and the kissing started and wouldn't stop. Lisa moved from the bench to the ground and got the same treatment, climbed on her and gave kisses.

I was surprised and amazed but extremely thankful for what I was watching. My little girl had suddenly lost her fear of people. I had to leave before the session was over, but below is what I sent out later that evening.

I want to thank all of you for what happened with Max today. It was a thing of beauty to watch, and we have pictures to prove it. As John has been saying, he believes there is so much potential here, and for once, John and I agree on something! Sorry, John, I couldn't resist!

My little girl doesn't need me anymore, but that won't keep me from visiting her.

Again, thank you all for these precious moments!

The next big event for her is when she walks out the door. Two weeks later.

Certainly, no surprise, she has been fostered and later adopted. An older couple took her and just called in to say she was on his lap. I believe I commented early on that I believed she could be a lap dog.

She came a long way in a short time. When you handle dogs like this, you can feel the tension in their bodies and can also feel as that tension melts away and the big TRUST word begins to happen. She stopped licking her lips, and her eyes became very soft, often closing them while I was handling and petting her.

This has been one of the most rewarding experiences I have had with a shelter dog, and I will never forget her.

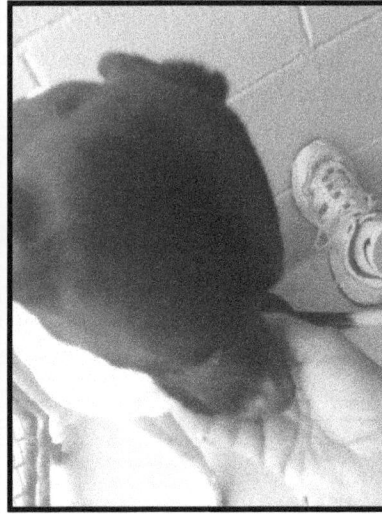

67

Chapter 21

Banjo

This is the story of a stray dog that was named Banjo by the Humane Society of Bertie County in Windsor North Carolina.

I was doing some volunteer time at the Hatteras Island Pet Resort, and in a conversation with Katie, the owner, she stated she had some items collected that she wanted to donate to Bertie County. Bertie is a rather remote shelter and, in the past, could always use food, towels, blankets, and so on to maintain their dog and cat residents. They are a small shelter and are lacking in some of the basic requirements that most shelters have. They don't have a washing machine, so soiled articles are thrown out. The cat area has HVAC, but the dog area has no A/C and recently had one heater installed to heat the whole kennel area that is closed in with plastic sheeting. The shelter is due for a remodeling but not sure when that will happen.

They call themselves a high-kill shelter as animals don't move through very quickly. I believe it is fair to say that rescues play an important part in saving animals in this shelter.

I decided to take Katie's items for Bertie and deliver them myself because Katie is extremely busy, and making time to do this would be difficult for her.

Before we made the trip there, I looked at the Bertie County website and found a very nicely done video on a dog named Banjo. Banjo was a stray that had been picked up in mid-December, and no one had inquired about him. His video showed him as a beautiful, soft-eyed dog that was very friendly.

Lisa Sharp was very kind and made the two-plus-hour drive with me, and we arrived a little early, and no one was there. We killed a little time, and shortly, Victoria was on site. We unloaded all the supplies and then moved to the kennel area, where we met Banjo. He was let out and ran around a little but soon settled down and allowed Lisa and me to get some hands-on time with him, and he responded beautifully. I had already cleared his rescue with John, providing we didn't see something of concern. He was great with us and other dogs also. There was another dog of interest, but another rescue group was interested in her, so we didn't interfere with that decision.

Soon, we had Banjo loaded up and were on our way back to Manteo. He traveled very well, and we arrived without incident. He was brought into receiving, where he was given shots, looked over, and checked for heartworm. Unfortunately, he tested positive for heartworm, and that was to be dealt with.

We have had some of these rescue dogs adopted quickly, and Banjo was no exception. A couple in a travel trailer, a quite nice one from what I understand, somehow discovered Banjo. They took him on foster to adopt and came back within a couple of days and adopted him.

As strange as this may seem, Banjo and his new owners were met on the beach by an employee of the Hatteras Island Pet Resort, and Banjo was recognized from pictures that we had sent out on him. He was also spotted in PetSmart by one of our Facebook users, and they met the new owners and said what nice people they were. We also found out that they were headed to Key West before heading to their home in Anchorage, Alaska.

So Banjo will be a road warrior for a while before settling into his new home up north. Needless to say, we are all very happy for Banjo, and it couldn't happen to a nicer dog. From wandering the streets as a stray that nobody wanted to be loved like this must be every dog's dream. Sleep and dream well, little buddy. You deserve it!

Update! I was contacted by Jackie Gibbs, saying that Banjo had been to their vet's office and received his shots for heartworm treatment. Also, they would be in the area for a while. I was given their names and decided to try and reach them. After a week or so, we made contact and exchanged e-mail messages with Donna. She said they had changed his name to Charlie, and he was doing extremely well.

They will be leaving the area in mid-February and heading to the West Coast before heading north to Alaska. Charlie has adjusted very well and loves his new mom and dad. They are very grateful to have found him and thanked us for rescuing him.

Looking back on this now, Lisa and I feel very good about our trip to Bertie County.

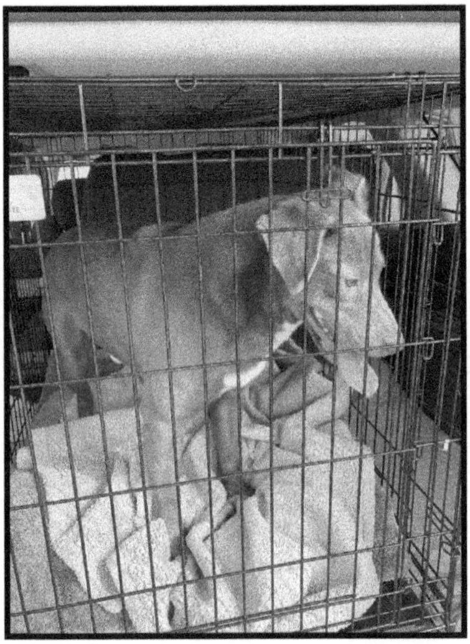

Chapter 22

The Puppy That Would

Our vet on the Virginia Eastern Shore, the Eastern Shore Animal Hospital, has a huge heart and has taken in many hard-case dogs. Remember Longshot, Stella, Lucas, and the list could go on and on.

This little story is truly remarkable. Some very young puppies, still nursing but without the mom, ended up at the vet's office. They were dehydrated, and their body systems were starting to shut down. In a desperate attempt to save them, staff went to work.

Someone even suggested that animal control be called on an outside chance that there was a mom there, nursing a litter. As miracles would have it, there was an older mom there with her litter, They were brought to the animal hospital in hopes that Mom would accept this failing puppy.

Again, as miracles would have it, she did, and today the puppy is alive and well. As wild as this all seems, the puppy is about the same age as the others, and you cannot tell him apart from the rest of the litter.

These guys are about six and a half weeks old, and I am working on placing them now. OBX is full and probably will be for a while, so I am in contact with another possible facility. Also, a four- or five-month-old needs to be placed.

I will keep everyone posted on what happens here.

An update on this, the puppies were brought to OBX, and all were quickly adopted. As for Mom, she was an older gal, and although I offered to pay to have her spayed, the vet took it upon themselves to do it, and she was moved to a wonderful rescue in Delaware. A very happy ending for all the survivors.

Chapter 23

Sissy

I saw Sissy on the Bertie County website and saw that her time was running out. Not much was known about her as she was picked up as a stray. She was at the city shelter, not the county shelter, which is considerably smaller than the county shelter. There is no staff there, but a deputy stops by once a day to feed and clean the four kennels. The feeding and cleaning are done with the dogs remaining in the kennels if they are full as there are no outside yards. The kennels are very small, and the dogs never leave the kennels.

When I met her, she was a very sweet dog. We were able to expose her to another dog that was there, and there were no aggression issues.

OBX SPCA was full, but I was able to pull her and board her until space was available at the SPCA. Within a couple of weeks, she was brought to the SPCA and adopted shortly thereafter.

Bertie County Humane Society

February 8

RESCUED!
🎉🎉HUGE THANKS TO OBX SPCA for saving SISSY ❤️❤️
———————————
🐶❤️SISSY is in the town of Windsor, NC SHELTER
SISSY NEEDS A RESCUE OR AN APPROVED HOME ASAP! 🪦🪦
#saveSissy

She sits alone in a kennel 24/7. 😔

This shelter is only a few doors down from the Bertie County Animal Shelter. They only have four kennels there. If they get full and need space, then they unfortunately euthanize for space. It would be such a travesty if Sissy lost her life due to no one adopting or rescuing her. She is a very sweet dog.

Sissy came in as a stray and was never reclaimed. We have met her, and she is extremely sweet. Sissy even met a very young child and really loved her. She was so good with the little girl. We do not know how she would be with other dogs as they have no way to test them there, and as we all know, it's not a fair assessment of dogs to be introduced while in a stressful environment. They do not have volunteers who walk their dogs every day, nor do the dogs get out for any exercise or a break from the kennel. We know Sissy has now been there for at least over a month and a half. ❤️

❤️We had her heartworm tested, and the vet said she is light heartworm positive, 😔 but she is Ehrlichia and Lyme negative. If you could find it in your heart to donate for her, we can help her, or a rescue could help her.

❤️PLEASE COME MEET SISSY! She is a beautiful and very sweet girl. Visits will have to be by appointment only. We have to coordinate with their shelter.

——————

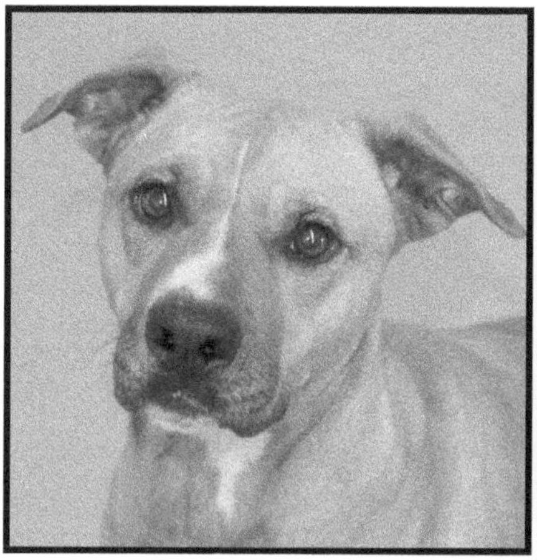

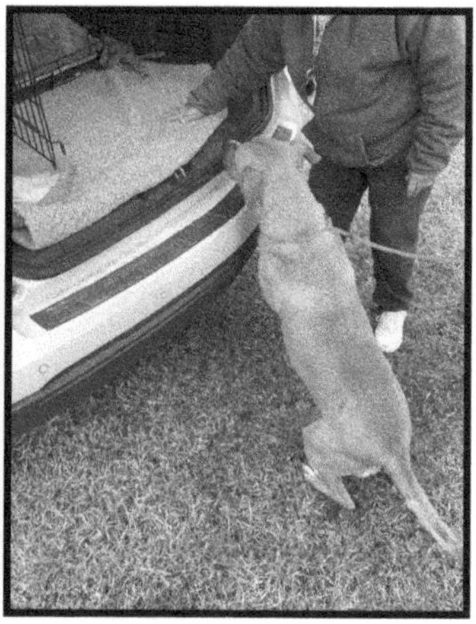

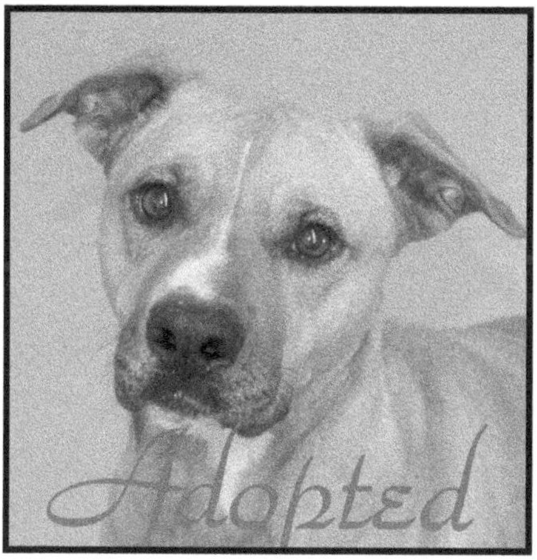
Adopted

Chapter 24

Diamond and Blitz

I was contacted by Eastern Shore Animal Control about two very sweet dogs whose time was running out on the Eastern Shore facility.

It seems someone got evicted from their residence and left two dogs chained up in the backyard. Luckily, animal control had been watching these dogs as a possible cruelty situation, so it was quickly recognized that the owner had disappeared. The dogs we taken in by A/C and waited at the facility for a possible adoption.

The dogs were a four-year-old tan female looking like a Lab/Pit mix named Diamond and about a year-and-a-half-old Blue Pit mix male named Blitz.

I was contacted about a week before their euthanasia date of January 31, 2018, to see if I could help place these dogs as all other attempts had failed. Everyone was full, and the dogs were nearing the end of their stay. Staff at the facility were really scrambling as they felt these were exceptional dogs and deserved a chance.

I contacted a local Pit Bull rescue that was a foster-based rescue and got them on the list for possible placement but was also told there were currently no vacancies.

I called my former shelter, the VB SPCA, and asked for help. After a couple of days, I received the message, saying, "We will take them."

I quickly contacted Susan Burdge of ESRAC and told her we had a rescue, and two days before running out of time, arrangements were made to transport the dogs.

Suzanne, who lives in Berlin, Maryland, did the transporting, and I decided to meet her at the SPCA to make sure there was no confusion as to what was happening. Everything went very well, and the dogs were received in, and the paperwork was handled, and Suzanne and I were on our way back home, in opposite directions.

Next step for these two will be getting up to date medically, some training, and placed up for adoption. Hopefully, this will end well for both these dogs.

CHAPTER 25

Diesel, Rosa, and Katie

On May 30, I was supposed to pick up a female Pit mix that I had never seen but was told about that I had named Katie. My usual procedure is to show up at Eastern Shore Animal Control at around eight thirty in the morning, load up, and be down to the Outer Banks SPCA by noontime.

There was some kind of communication mix-up because I waited for forty-five minutes, and no one showed up. I had been talking with a local rescue person about a couple of Pit mixes that she wanted relocated, so I called her, and we met at Walmart for the transfer. I had an OBX SPCA vehicle, so I was able to take both of them, Rosa and Diesel. Both great dogs, with Rosa being a little dog selective. I felt badly leaving Katie behind, but I had to get on the road.

Both these dogs were dogs that were on chains. Diesel was surrendered to the rescue, but she had to pay $350 for Rosa and four of her puppies.

The trip down was uneventful as was going through receiving. Both dogs were already up to date on shots and were very clean as they were living indoors.

This turned out to be a difficult adjustment for these dogs as they were living in a house. Going from that environment to a kennel environment, no matter how good the shelter is, is a very stressful process. In Diesel's case, it was so stressful that our Director asked that

81

I return him. As it turns out, the rescue person that I got them from had an older daughter that wanted Diesel but couldn't take him where she was previously living but moved during that two weeks, so Diesel went right into an adoption. We were delighted for him.

Rosa was handling the kennel well and was soon fostered. The young man who had her also had some foreign people living with him, and they turned out to be afraid of Rosa, so she was returned. At the time of this writing, she was handling kennel life well and just waiting for her turn for another chance. She is an absolutely beautiful dog.

This brings us back to Katie. The Eastern Shore Animal Control facility procedures call for dogs to be held for eight days. An additional seven days after are allowed, but after that, they are to be euthanized.

Staffs at this facility do their best to find homes for these dogs. They call rescues, but Pits are very hard to place. The local SPCA will not take any Pits or anything that looks like it may have Pit in it, so opportunities on the Shore for placement of these dogs are pretty slim.

I received a message from A/C staff that Katie needed to get out ASAP. I had been asked to hold off bringing any more dogs to the Outer Banks SPCA because they were full. My safety valve, of the local vet, was also full. I reached out to a local facility that had called themselves a Sanctuary, when they first started up a few years ago. This was my last hope of placing her temporarily while we waited for an opening at the Outer Banks SPCA. The facility is called Ocean Sands. Arrangements were made, and I picked her up, and we headed to the Outer Banks SPCA, where she would be received in and get her shots before being transferred to Ocean Sands. As it turns out, there had been some fostering and adopting activity, so we had room for Katie at the SPCA.

Katie was an instant hit with everyone. She loved everyone, and everyone loved her. She started smiling when she went out of my truck and, five days later, still has that smile on her face.

She is a big girl, overweight, and shows signs of having many litters of puppies. Her story was that she was used for the puppies and was eventually turned loose. A/C picked her up and knew where her owner was, but when contacted, he said he didn't want her anymore. That was a good thing.

So Katie belonged to the Outer Banks SPCA and was soon adopted. See pictures below.

Chapter 26

Charlie Girl

We were living on the Virginia Eastern Shore, and on our way to town, we passed by a house that had been feeding a stray dog. She was an unsprayed female and eventually had a litter of puppies. When the puppies were old enough to start running around and playing in the yard, they were noticed by people passing by, and soon, most of them got adopted.

One of the puppies was leery of people and would not allow anyone to get too close. I stopped and talked with the folks who owned the property, and our concern of her getting hit by a car was mutual. They started to let her in on the porch and started to feed her. The idea was that they would lock her in, and I would be able to get her and bring her to the SPCA.

The plan worked beautifully, and I was able to move her to an SPCA. I named her Charlie Girl, and she was adopted within a week or so.

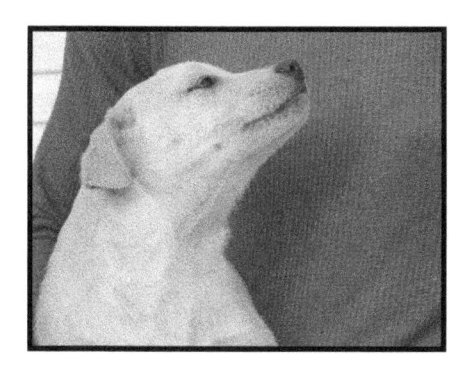

Chapter 27

Puppy Litter Number 1

Another litter was born to the stray dog that was being fed off a main road going into town. The concern was these dogs would get hit by a car as they got old enough to start playing in the yard. I was notified by the property owner that another litter was born under the shed in their backyard. We waited until they were weaned and moving around the yard and decided the best way to catch them would be to use dog traps. We placed the food on one end of the trap, and as they entered the trap, they stepped on a plate that released the action and closed the door behind them.

We started the trapping, and within a couple of days, we had all five puppies, beautiful healthy puppies that were brought down to the OBX SPCA, and all were adopted very quickly.

The property owners stopped feeding the mother dog, and she disappeared. I would have loved to trap her and gotten her spayed but not sure if she was too feral to be adopted.

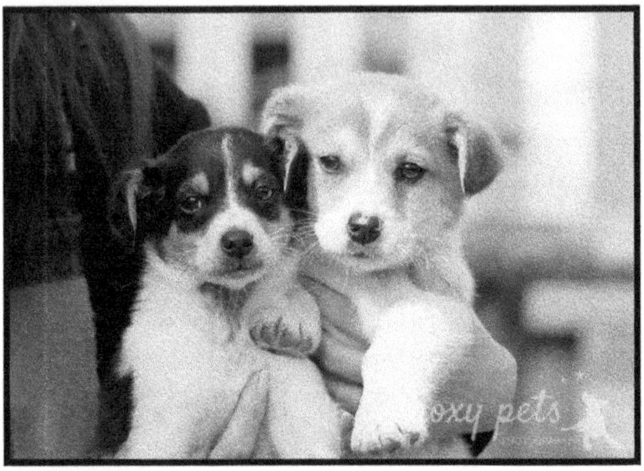

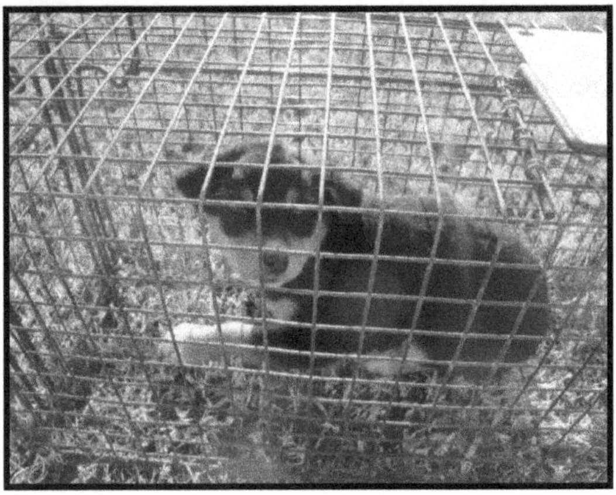

Chapter 28

Puppy Litter Number 2

This second litter was born a couple of towns away. The mother had found an upside-down wheelbarrow and burrowed under it and gave birth. Very clever Mom as the puppies were protected from the elements and anything else that came their way. The property owners noticed her activity and figured out what was going on. I was called, and we discussed the situation, and it was decided that when they noticed the puppies playing in the yard, they would gather them up and call me. They were making a habit of handling the puppies, so they were used to human contact.

The plan worked well, and the puppies were transferred to the OBX SPCA, where they were adopted quite quickly.

Chapter 29

Animal Control Rescue Dogs

The following dogs were mainly Pit Bull mixes that were picked up as strays and were in the custody of animal control on the Virginia Eastern Shore. As previously stated, we worked out an arrangement. If the dog's temperament permitted, we would visit the dog and decide if he would be a candidate for a transfer to the OBX SPCA. I would do this along with staff at animal control.

Among these dogs were Billy, Lacey, Prada, Clyde, Luke, Hank, Darby, and Scrappy. All these dogs found homes through the OBX SPCA with the exception of Scrappy. He had an advance case of heartworm and could not be saved. As far as I know, he is the only rescue that had to be euthanized for any reason out of all these dogs.

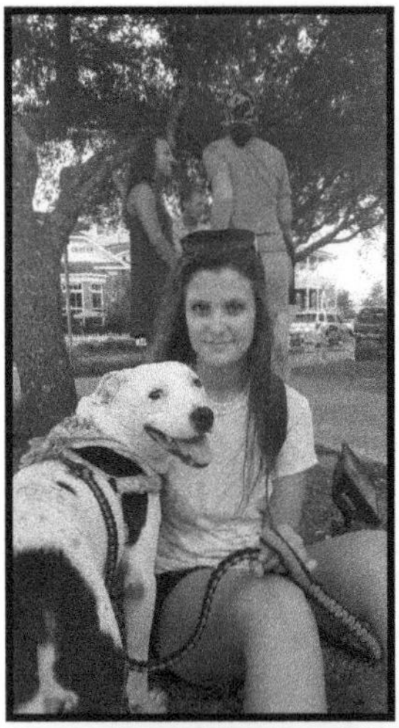
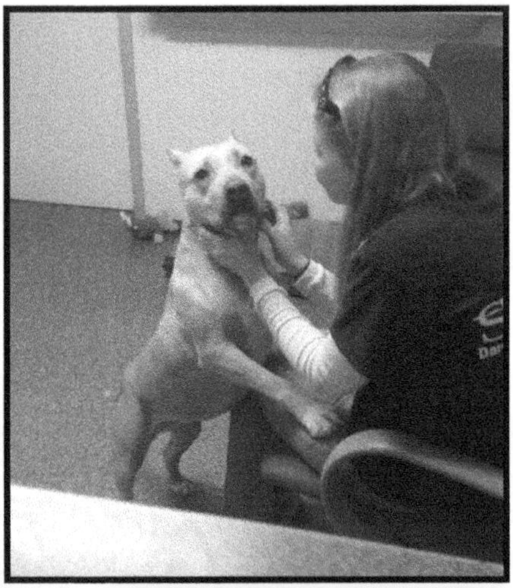
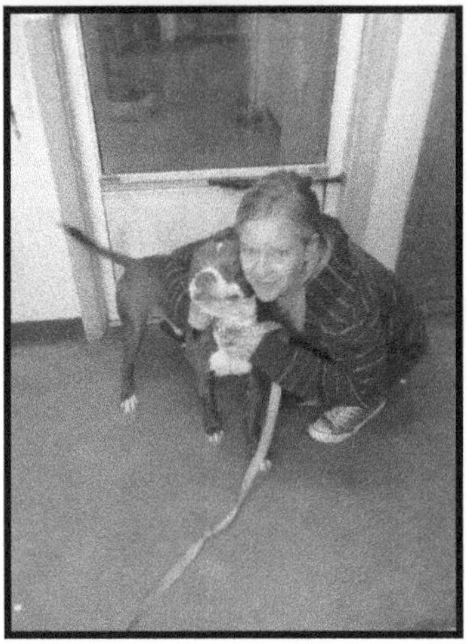
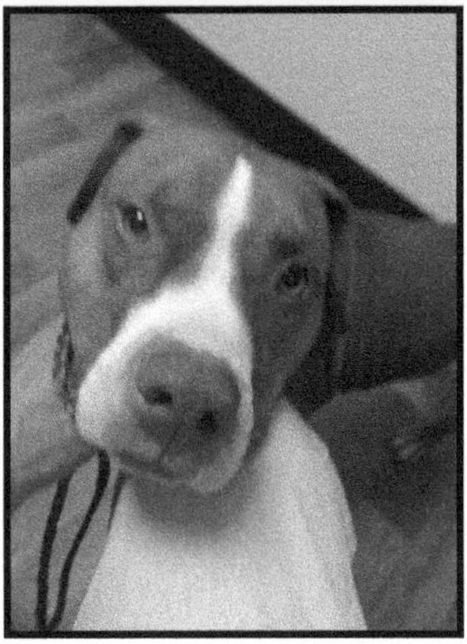

Lightning Source UK Ltd.
Milton Keynes UK
UKHW010521100320
359866UK00020B/39/J